Something's Happening Here

Something's Happening Here

A Sixties Odyssey from Brooklyn to Woodstock

Mark Berger

ee

excelsior editions

STATE UNIVERSITY OF NEW YORK PRESS
Albany, NY

Author photo (back cover): Anthony Tassarotti. www.tassarotti.com.

My memoir consists of stories that I have recreated from my recollections. I have tried to be as accurate as I can, but I am well aware that memory is imperfect. To protect the privacy of the people I knew, I have changed their names and some identifying characteristics. Please allow me one conceit: it was in December 1969, four months after Woodstock, that BB King gave Hugh Romney the nickname Wavy Gravy. It is how he has been known since and how I refer to him in the book.

Published by State University of New York Press, Albany

Printed in the United States of America

Excelsior Editions is an imprint of State University of New York Press

For information, contact State University of New York Press, Albany, NY
www.sunypress.edu

Library of Congress Cataloging-in-Publication Data

Names: Berger, Mark, 1945– author.
Title: Something's happening here : a sixties odyssey from Brooklyn to Woodstock / Mark Berger.
Other titles: Sixties odyssey from Brooklyn to Woodstock
Description: Albany, NY : Excelsior Editions, an imprint of State University of New York Press, [2019]
Identifiers: LCCN 2018033273 | ISBN 9781438474625 (pbk. : alk. paper) | ISBN 9781438474632 (ebook)
Subjects: LCSH: Berger, Mark, 1945– | Hippies—United States—Biography. | Counterculture—United States—Biography. | Youth—United States—Social life and customs—20th century. | Woodstock Festival (1969 : Bethel, N.Y.)— Anecdotes. | Young men—United States—Biography. | Coming of age. | Bohemianism—New York (State)—New York—History—20th century. | Baby boom generation—New York (State)—Biography. | Brooklyn (New York, N.Y.)—Biography.
Classification: LCC HQ799.7 .B47 2019 | DDC 305.5/680092 [B] —dc23
LC record available at https://lccn.loc.gov/2018033273

10 9 8 7 6 5 4 3 2 1

To Rain

THE LOVE OF MY LIFE
AND MY DAILY INSPIRATION

Contents

Acknowledgments

I want to thank Marion Roach Smith, memoirist, teacher, and friend, whose generosity, wisdom, and support provided the environment where I found my voice as a storyteller.

Marion introduced me to my editor, the witty, erudite, and charming Rob Brill. Rob helped me turn a promising manuscript into one that was worthy of publication.

My thanks to James Peltz, the affable and knowledgeable codirector editor of SUNY Press, who honored me with a book contract and the opportunity to add my work to the estimable SUNY Press/Excelsior Editions catalogue. Thanks also, to Eileen Nizer, Senior Production Editor and Michael Campochiaro, Senior Promotions Manager who have turned this manuscript into a book and then sent it out to the world.

From my first memoir stories, Randall Jones, my brother-in-law, a talented wordsmith with a background in book publishing, encouraged me and believed in the validity and viability of my stories. I am deeply grateful for his many insights and brotherhood.

To Richard Strauss whose wisdom and support have been invaluable.

Thanks to my attorney Denise Gibbon at Abovetheline.com who provided me with helpful and practical legal advice.

A bow to my dear friend Larry Reilly whose long experience in advertising has helped me to understand SEO and other necessary promotional strategies.

To all the people in my book—dear friends, friends, lovers, acquaintances and adversaries: while our paths went off in divergent directions, I am grateful you were all a part of my story. Each and every turn my journey has taken has brought me to this moment.

Last, I am grateful to Samuel and Rose Blume Berger, my parents, both of whom died many years ago. You instilled in me the importance of integrity and hard work, but I had to find my own way out of the wilderness.

Prologue

We stop at the crest overlooking the stage. While I could probably finesse our way back into the press section like I did last night, it doesn't feel right. Once is enough. Moving through the crowd, we sit down maybe a football field away.

Onstage, the band is finishing up a song. The lead singer has on a long-sleeve tie-dyed T-shirt.

"Who's playing?" I ask a girl seated next to us.

"Joe Cocker."

We shrug our shoulders.

"He's English," the girl continues and passes us a joint.

The band starts playing "Just Like a Woman." Cocker sings the opening line "Nobody feels any pain" and he sounds like he's an alumni of the Ray Charles School of Singing, and like Brother Ray, he sings behind the beat. While Dylan's original is a scornful picture of a former lover, Cocker's full-bodied voice tells a tale of a heart filled with anguish. The music takes him away. Us too.

Joanie and I exchanges smiles, she leans against my chest. I put my arms around her shoulders, drawing her head alongside mine, tousling her hair.

The organ plays two notes, and a murmur undulates through the crowd. We all know this one. It's "With A Little Help from My

Friends," from *Sergeant Pepper*, a record I bet every single person here owns and knows by heart.

Unlike the little ditty that Ringo croons, Cocker sings as if his life depends on it. He wails the lyrics incoherently, whirling his right arm playing an invisible guitar, staggering, vibrating, almost collapsing, then resurrecting himself. He's testifying, telling it like it is: "I get by with a little help from my friends."

A little help from my friends? I'm hip. Cocker's turning the Beatles' song into an anthem. It's about all of us here at Woodstock. How has everyone gotten through all the bummers—the chaos, traffic jams, thunderstorms, the hunger, the heat, all the rotten conditions? How? With a little help from our friends—a shared sandwich here, a laugh, a sip of water there, a toke, a free meal, a smile, a kiss, a hug.

When Joe Cocker finishes, people rise to their feet and pump their fists in the air. And, as if on cue, the skies go from gray to black. Storm clouds rush in. One upon another, lightning bolts flash like strobes—freezing the crowd's upturned heads, open mouths, outstretched arms, and then, thunderclaps explode and torrential rain renders our bowl-shaped metropolis once more a flooded city.

"Here we go again," I say, grabbing Joanie's hand. "Let's move quick."

TOWN HILL

Problem is Zooby and I are underage. The solution is getting past Rodney Jenkins, the bouncer at Town Hill, so we've invited Billy along. Since Rodney and Billy played football together at Erasmus Hall High, we're hoping for old times' sake, plus some grease, the doors of the nightclub will swing open for us. For Billy, the deal is sweet—he gets us in and the show's on us.

Town Hill features the best R&B and doo-wop singers: from Dinah Washington to Sam Cooke, from the Platters to the Drifters. It's the coolest place. Tonight the great Earl "Speedo" Carroll, former lead singer of the Cadillacs, is debuting with the Coasters.

Handing Billy a ten-spot, I say, "You got the ball, now get us over the line."

When Rodney sees Billy, he goes, "Hey, my man, hear 'Rasmus lost to Tilden. Should be ashamed of themselves."

"Never happened when we played, Jenkins. We had the team."

"Ain't that the truth." They slap each other five while Billy slips him the ten. Jenkins nods and in we go.

Over the buzz of the jukebox, boisterous laughter and conversation fill the Hill. Cigarette smoke creates a silvery, chiffon ambience. The room is swaying.

The maître d' leads us to a table in the back near the horseshoe-shaped bar. When our waitress arrives, Billy orders a beer. Attempting to project some hipness, Zooby and I order rum and coke. Two black couples are at the next table, the guys, in pastel jackets and open-collared shirts, have their arms draped over the shoulders of their dates who are wearing tight, short dresses with plunging necklines.

"Man, those cats dress so cool," Billy whispers.

"They're dressed to party. We look like we're going to temple," I say.

"We've reached the promised land," Zooby adds.

Almost as proof, Billy leans in and nods toward the bar, "There he is—Speedo."

Sure enough, laughing it up with some people is Earl Carroll, Mr. Cool.

The curtain opens with Big Al Sears and the band getting into the groove with rocking renditions of "Night Train" and "Honky Tonk."

The emcee announces, "Ladies and gentlemen, direct from the land of the pyramids where she drove the Nile wild, the dancer who makes the mummies murmur for more, the one, the only, Little Egypt."

With the band playing "Satin Doll," Little Egypt, dressed all in gold, gyrates onto the stage, wearing a halter top, a skirt with slits to her hips, and arms coiled in bracelets. Her skin is a shimmering gold and her body's beyond beyond.

Shimmying and shaking, twirling and whirling, strutting and stripping, she mesmerizes every guy in the joint. Undressing to the legal limit, she hesitates. The crowd urges her on, and just as it seems she's going to give in, she throws a kiss and dashes offstage.

The lights go up. It takes a while for the crowd to settle down. The Coasters are next.

We're astonished, speechless.

Finally, Billy says, "Let's get another round."

Seeing our waitress talking with the bartender, I volunteer to give her our order. Moving toward the bar, I notice a chick in a tight skirt and even tighter top moving my way. I realize it's Little Egypt.

Why not be bold? My voice climbs a register or two. "Miss Egypt, can I buy you a drink?"

Several bar patrons turn. Earl Carroll, his smile gone, rises deliberately from his stool. I hear Billy say, "Mark's a dead man." It hits me, oh, no, she's Speedo's girl.

Stopping a foot from me, Little Egypt slowly looks me up and down, pauses, and, in a stage whisper, says, "Sonny . . . when I want a baby, I'll have one."

The bar erupts with laughter. Speedo's smiling too. I sit down trying my best to become invisible. When the waitress appears, I order coffee.

The emcee introduces the Coasters, featuring Earl "Speedo" Carroll. Coming onstage in green tuxedos, they belt out "Charlie Brown." The audience is all theirs, mouthing the words to their hits like "Under the Boardwalk," "Poison Ivy" and the doo-wop classic, "Zing Went the Strings of My Heart." The guys next to us are holding their ladies close and rocking back and forth. Pure fun.

Afterwards, walking in the cool night air down Eastern Parkway, I tell my pals, "I'm not sorry I did it. I'd rather be bold than boring."

Zooby puts in his two cents. "Do what the Coasters do: first they learn the song, then they sing it."

April 1962

OFF AND ON

It's after midnight, cold and rainy, and I've got some time to kill. Since the beginning of my senior year of high school, I make it a point never to go home on a weekend night before one a.m. Home? If that means a place you want to go back to, there's no way I can call the one-bedroom apartment I share with my parents and brother home.

Ducking into the doorway of Blynn's drugstore on Church and 7th, I light a Camel. As I take the first drag, a black-and-white crawls by. Staring right at me, the cop riding shotgun says something to his partner who glances in my direction. Not wanting to get hassled, I tug up my bomber jacket collar, trudge the block to Ocean Parkway and march right past my apartment house.

Playing a little game, I ID parked cars by their tail fins or hubcaps. Without realizing it, I find myself searching for Buicks, especially one from the mid-1950s. *Off and on*, I think with a smile. In these cars, the ignition switch is set up so that the driver can remove the key in the On, Off or Lock position. The thing is, if the driver takes the key out in either On or Off, then all someone like me has to do is manually turn the switch and the car will start. No hot-wiring, no master key, nothing. Just get behind the wheel, flip the switch and go. Me and my pals have an inside joke—when someone asks one of us if we drive, we answer with a smirk, "Off and on."

If I find a car, will I really go for a joy ride? Probably. I feel this urgency to do things that prove I'm not going to follow the straight and narrow path my parents have taken. I'm not going to live the way they do.

The rain is working its magic—changing the September night into something more mysterious—hushing the street noise, creating gutter rainbows out of raindrops, streetlights, and motor oil and allowing me to move like a phantom.

Spying a black '53 Buick Special with a dent in the right rear fender, I peer in the passenger window and see the door lock button is up. I know, I just know. Quietly opening the door, I slide across to the driver's seat, crank down the window and flip out my cigarette. With my hand on the ignition switch, I take a deep breath and confirm to myself that if the engine turns over, I'm ready-teddy.

The motor roars. I come off the accelerator, turn on the lights and wipers, adjust the mirrors, rotate the steering wheel, check the street, give it gas, and pull away from the curb, feeling a potent mixture of excitement, freedom, and fear.

This '53 is slow and clumsy. Taking the first turn a little too wide, I struggle to straighten her out. Immediately ahead is a red traffic light. Jamming on the brakes, I barely miss smashing my head into the windshield. With my heart beating double-time, I tell myself, "Stay cool."

In a few blocks, I come to the quiet Albemarle Road section, with its tree-lined streets and fancy houses. It's dark and quiet here. But nothing lasts forever, least of all a Brooklyn neighborhood. Driving out of this section, I tool into the adjoining Ditmas neighborhood which has side-by-side apartment buildings. Even at this late hour, the streets are active—people head home from the subway, walk their dogs. Cars cruise for parking places.

Nervousness and fatigue are taking their toll. Making a turn, I notice all the cars are parked facing me. What's the matter with these jerks? In the distance, I see car lights headed my way. Shit, I'm the jerk. I'm going the wrong way on a one-way street. Quickly pulling over to a fire hydrant, I turn off my headlights, duck down and pray those car lights don't belong to the Man. Sneaking a peek, it's all clear. My left foot is twitching, my breath is jagged. Turning the Buick around so that I'm going the right way, I drive toward Albemarle Road, slip into a parking space, turn off the engine and stroll away with as much nonchalance as I can muster.

On Ocean Parkway, an ambulance with lights flashing races by. I picture myself inside on a stretcher going to Coney Island Hospital after driving that Buick smack into a head-on collision.

I see the cop who eyeballed me sitting next to me and I'm in handcuffs.

Joy ride? Who thought that one up? There's no joy for me in Flatbush tonight. Lighting another cigarette, I check my watch. It's a quarter to two. I can go home now.

September 1961

BIRD

"You look like someone died," I say to Harold, as I slide into the back booth at Barney's Luncheonette.

"They took Bird away."

"Who? The cops?"

"No, his parents. They bought a house on Long Island without telling him and yesterday morning they moved everything, including him. He snuck a call to me to let me know."

"I bet they did it for his mom's tweety birds," I say.

"Probably that too. She's nuts about those feathered fuckers. But they told him it's 'cause he's cutting school all the time, staying out all hours, hanging around with bums like us. Y'know, the usual stuff."

"Remember that time back in ninth grade. We went over to his house to play cards and the place was filled with chirping. Man, what a racket."

"That's when we stopped calling him Douglas and started calling him Bird and the name stuck," Harold says. "He's kind of turned into one—dresses to the nines, always preening himself, and, come to think about it, he flits around."

"Harold, don't sweat it," I say. "Bird'll be back."

～

Two weeks later, there's Bird and Harold at Barney's, with their hair slicked back and leather jacket collars turned up.

"Mark, how 'bout coming out to the island with Harold for the weekend?" Bird asks.

"It's bad? Huh."

"Worse than bad. Can you picture yourself being in jail and your mother's the warden? I used to be jealous of all the attention she gave her canaries, now I see I was the lucky one. She said she'll let Harold stay over if he comes with someone she likes, like you."

"Me? What'd I ever do for her to like me?"

"Our mothers played mahjong together, that's why. Anyway, come on, we'll have fun. We'll go to the Roosevelt Field Shopping Center."

I don't really want to go, but looking at these two best friends together, I can't say no. Friday evening, Harold and I are on the Long Island Rail Road to Woodmere.

Next afternoon, Mrs. Harris drops us off at the shopping center. Bird tells his mom we'll take a bus back home. After a bit of window shopping, a sneaky grin works its way across Harold's face.

"Let's go to Jones Beach."

"It's October, no one'll be there," I say.

"Then that's the place for us," Bird goes. "C'mon, Mark, it's a short drive."

Short drive? Oh, I get it, they planned this from the get-go.

"I don't appreciate being tricked into things," I mutter. But I'm in.

The parking lot is packed. We spread out and start checking out cars to boost. I'm hoping we strike out, but no such luck. In no time, Bird is inside a blue '59 Bonneville. He ducks under the dashboard, starts it up and pulls out. We hop in and off we go.

Cruising down a store-lined street, I ask, "You know how to get to the beach?"

"Not really," replies Bird, "Maybe there's a map, look in the glove compartment."

To keep the sun out of his eyes, he pulls down the visor. Clipped to its inner side is an official Hempstead police department parking pass.

Harold shouts, "Holy shit, this is a cop's car."

Distracted, Bird doesn't see that the car in front of us has stopped. He tail-ends it. Crunch.

"What now?" I say.

Bird seems undaunted. "Follow me and don't panic."

Getting out of the car, he goes to other driver, a woman in her twenties. She's shaken, but unhurt.

Establishing eye contact, he says, "I'm so sorry. My dad's a police officer. He's in the store back there. I'll get him. He'll take care of everything."

She nods and pulls to the curb. Pedestrians are watching.

Confidently, Bird walks in the direction we came from. We follow. Passing one store, two, three, our gait quickens.

Hitting the corner, Bird hisses, "Let's split." Bolting through alleyways, crossing backyards, hopping fences, we keep going and going, listening for police sirens all the way. Finally, we reach a main drag and stop to catch our breath.

"All we have to do is get to the train station," Bird says.

At a stoplight, he approaches a pickup, but it drives off.

A roofing company truck filled with construction debris pulls up. Bird says something to the driver, hands him some bills, then waves to us. We climb up and in with the junk. Ten minutes later, we arrive at the Lawrence LIRR station.

Trying to act like we're not together, we buy our tickets separately and sit apart. At last, the train arrives. We glance around; the station's quiet. Onboard, we sit down together.

I'm disgusted with this whole escapade. First, with the two of them for conning me. But mostly with myself, for going along when I didn't want to.

"Bird," I say, "that was stupid. We were real lucky today."

"I know," he says. "I'm trying to find something, I keep searching, but this ain't it."

As we pull into Woodmere, they get up, but I stay seated.

"I'm going back to Brooklyn. Tell your mother I'm allergic to birds."

October 1961

Bouncing down the long staircase from Sam's Pool Room to Church Avenue, I'm feeling good. Paulie D'Amico lost to me in nine ball and I got five bucks to prove it.

Passing Barney's, where we hang out, I see Bird and Harold leaning against a red and white '59 Ford Fairlane. Harold, with his dark hair slicked back, is wearing a gray, striped button down and black slacks. Bird is dressed in green, glen-plaid pants and a corn-colored Italian knit shirt. Smooth. The sun's setting, but he's got on Ray-Bans.

"Bird, what's with the shades?" I ask.

"Eric's back in town," he answers mysteriously.

"Eric?"

"Y'know, Eric, the beatnik," Harold says. "He's back from San Francisco."

Lifting his shades, Bird winks and giggles. "And I'm weedy glad he is."

"Be cool, man," rasps Harold.

"You best be cool, too."

"I want in," I say. "Thunderbird's disgusting. Booze don't do it for me."

Harold looks both ways. "Not everyone can handle pot. It's powerful shit. Before you go 'Me too,' think about it."

"I just did. All the cats at Town Hill smoke grass. Besides, I need something, I'm totally depressed. Supposed to start college in the fall, but I hate school. Hate it. Anyway, I just took a fin from Paulie up at Sam's." Waving the five dollar bill, I add, "I'm buying."

"Gimme a sec," says Harold, who goes into the luncheonette to make the call.

Returning a minute later, he goes, "Eric says he ain't into virgins, so you're gonna need to make up some kind of story."

As the street lights come on, we stride the couple of blocks over to a two-family home off Caton Avenue. Answering the door, Eric, sporting a goatee, is wearing cut-offs and a faded blue work shirt. A blaring TV fills the living room with laughter and applause.

"Hello, Mrs. Byrnes," Harold calls out. " 'The Andy Williams Show,' right? My mom's in love with him."

"Tell Eleanor," Mrs. Byrnes replies, "I'm first in line."

In Eric's room, Billie Holiday is on one wall and bookshelves fill the other. Looking at me dead on, he says, "Harold said you smoked before."

"Yeah, at Town Hill, y'know, that nightclub up on Eastern Parkway," I say, passing him the money. "I'm cool."

Eric reaches under his pillow, pulls out a couple of one-by-three inch envelopes and tosses them on the bed. Bird fingers them and selects one.

Seeing us out, Eric whispers, "Remember to forget where this came from. *Ciao.*"

Back on the street, I'm stunned. "That's all five bucks buys? That little envelope. I thought we'd get a bagful."

Harold ignores me. "I got rolling papers. Let's go up to my roof."

We turn the corner of Caton Avenue and head into his apartment building, taking the elevator to the sixth floor and hiking up the last flight. Bird leans back and stares into a night sky filled with glimmering stars and blinking airplane lights. "That's where I'd like to be."

Putting some pot on a cigarette paper, Harold rolls a joint that's thin at the ends and like a small marble in the middle.

"OK, watch us. You take a toke and hold it in for as long as you can."

Flipping his Zippo, Harold lights the joint, inhales deeply, holds his breath, and then coughs. Bird does exactly the same thing, as do I.

After several hits, I ask, "What now?"

"Now is now," says Bird.

Slowly, a lightness filters into my head. My body relaxes. It feels cool. I feel cool.

"We can't stay here," Harold says. "The bozos on the sixth floor will hear us walking around."

"Let's go to Prospect Park," says Bird. "It'll be nice and quiet."

So off we go to Park Circle, uncharacteristically crossing with the light. Lampposts sparkle on the tree-lined paths, cars hum on the park drive.

"How long's it last?"

"Not long enough," Bird says.

"So that's it. I like it. Man, I kinda feel tall. How 'bout you guys?"

"That's why it's called getting high. Dig?" says Harold.

"High as the moon," giggles Bird.

"Now I know why the Man in the Moon just smiles and keeps his big mouth shut."

We slap each other's hands and laugh.

July 1962

BECK'S BUSY BEE

At Beck's Busy Bee Grocery, here's how it works. The phone rings, Mr. Beck answers it, writes down an order, saying, "Please," "Oh, it's my pleasure" and "Thank you" as many times as humanly possible. Then he hands me the slip.

"Fill it fast. They're waiting."

I amble around the store gathering the various items, which he totals up, stapling the slip in his customer's book and putting a duplicate in with the order.

"Colonel and Mrs. Wilcox on 56th Street, 15 minutes, no more."

Hoisting the box of groceries on my shoulder, I hit the street where the August sun, treeless sidewalks, and white brick buildings conspire to melt the soles of my sneakers.

"We cater to 'people of value,'" Mr. Beck often says, meaning the corporate bigwigs, movie stars, diplomats, millionaires, and heiresses who live in this Upper East Side enclave that proclaims their lofty status in two words: Sutton Place.

Running from 53rd to 59th Street, east of First Avenue, Sutton Place sits above the East River and just blocks from the United Nations and midtown Manhattan. Doormen, building superintendents, maids, chauffeurs, shopkeepers, beat cops, and delivery boys, like me, are at the residents' beck and call.

For the Wilcox order, I take the service elevator to their kitchen door and hand the box to their cook, an elderly black woman, who says, "Thank you, but ain't nobody home," meaning no tip this time, because her employers are out.

"That's OK." I say.

Walking back to the store, it hits me that I don't hear the sound of coins jingling in my pockets, which means I haven't made any money today. Six hours on the job, eight deliveries, no tips, not a one. I tell myself not to worry, it'll even out.

Back at the store, Mr. B. goes, "What'd you do to the Colonel's order?"

"Wha? Nothin'."

"Mrs. Wilcox just got home. When she opened the Wise potato chips, she found mostly broken ones. The Colonel's wife certainly can't serve her guests broken chips, can she?"

"Huh?"

"Who's right? The customer, one hundred percent of the time," says Mr. B. "For 16 years, that simple rule has kept the Busy Bee in business." Handing me two bags of chips, he sends me back. "Pronto, Tonto."

No point in defending myself. I need this summer job to pay for Driver's Ed in the fall, which will get me my license when I turn 17.

By six o'clock, I've made four more deliveries, 12 in all, and I've gotten zilch each and every time. Six-fifteen, another order, two boxes for Messina on 54th. I'll need the cart for this one. This customer is different from the others. He's like a playboy— cool dresser, cooler women, and by far my best tipper. He's a sure thing for two or three bucks.

C'mon. Mr. Messina, make it right.

After I place the boxes on his kitchen counter, Mr. Sure Thing gives me a self-conscious smile. "I didn't get to the bank today. Next time."

"Next time."

Just before closing time, the boss hands me a new order slip. "It's on 58th Street, the Wagners. You can go home from there."

Walking up First Avenue, there a bounce in my step. I start thinking this situation through. One measly quarter won't make up for a whole day of being stiffed, that's for sure. If I deliver 14 grocery orders in a single day and don't make a red cent, now that could be some sort of record.

I get serious. Let's say, they only give me a dime, do I still got a shot at the record? Nah, 'cause that's the difference between a one-hitter and a no-hitter—one-hitters don't count. OK. What if I do a little something to kind of mess up my chances? Uh-uh, that's cheating—only counts if I play it straight.

Ringing the Wagners' service bell, I hear a man and a woman laughing. No answer. I ring again. Footsteps approach, then, through the door, the man says, "Who's there?"

"Beck's Busy Bee."

"Leave the bags there, I'll get them later. Thanks."

"Oh, it's my pleasure, thank you," I say, just like Mr. B. would do.

That night at Barney's, our hangout, Zooby, Ronnie and Harold crack up as I take them through my miserable day—it's so pathetic, it's hysterical.

"Mark, tip money never lasts," Zooby says, "but you can keep a good story for a lifetime."

August 1961

On this sunny day in May, driving down Centre Street in Manhattan in my brother Paul's red '63 Corvair convertible with the top down, I'm feeling superfine. My buddy Billy is in front and two cute Jersey girls we just picked up in Washington Square Park are in the back seat. They accepted our invitation to celebrate July in May by going with us to Coney Island for a ride on the Cyclone, hot dogs at Nathan's, and a stroll on the boardwalk. Is the rollercoaster even open yet? Who knows? But so far, so good.

The Brooklyn Bridge is ahead. As I start across Chambers Street, a blue '59 Dodge jumps the red light and pulls dead ahead of me. Honking, I swerve left, but, for some reason, so does the Dodge, causing my front bumper to glance off his rear fender. Damn.

Pulling over a ways up the entrance ramp, I ask how everyone's doing. The girls are wide-eyed but say they're OK.

Always the jock, Billy goes, "I've taken harder hits from linebackers."

I inspect the damage: the bumper's crunched, but it didn't go into the front tire, so the car's drivable. What the hell am I going to tell my brother? Thankfully, he's gone for the week. I'll deal with that later.

I walk back to the intersection. Standing beside his Harley, watching me approach, is a motorcycle cop in mirrored shades.

"You saw it, right? That guy ran the red and jumped right in front of me," I say.

He shrugs his shoulders. I turn to look in the front window of the Dodge. The driver and his passenger, definitely his wife, are in their fifties and shaped like pears. He's bald with a small, dark mustache, and she's a peroxide blond with too much lipstick.

With his hands cupping the back of his head, the man moans, "My neck, my neck."

Between sobs, his wife shouts, "Oy, my back." They sound so rehearsed, I feel like applauding.

"It's your fault, you ran the red," I say, but no one's paying any attention to me.

The cop gets on his radio. I motion that I'm going to get my papers. He nods. I'm getting more aggravated by the second. I know how this dance goes—ambulances, police reports, lawsuits, and in the end, a big fat check for them and a gigantic pain in the ass for me.

Billy's alone at the curb. "Chicks went home. What's up, *Kimosabe*?"

"Get in, let's go."

Glancing back toward the corner, Billy hops in. Sliding behind the wheel, I start over the bridge. I weave through the traffic like a cab driver. Both of us just stare straight ahead—knowing we'll hear the Harley's siren before we see it. The bridge is only a mile across, but it feels more like ten.

Incredibly, we reach the Brooklyn side without incident. Taking the back streets, I pull to the curb when I get to Atlantic Avenue. I tell Billy he should get out, just in case.

"What happened back there?"

"We just tapped them, right? I go to see how they're doing and both of them are totally faking it, screaming their heads off—'My neck, my back.'"

"Phony bastards. I hate rip-off artists."

"Cop probably saw the whole thing, but if it's old farts versus us, who's he's gonna side with?"

"I dig," Billy says.

"My brother is only away for a couple of more days. I gotta get it fixed before he finds out."

"Hey, remember my friend Terry Mack? He's got a body shop across from Greenwood Cemetery. Go see him."

Billy turns and smiles. "Berger, you're something else. You know that? Go slow. Call me later."

Driving furtively, it takes 20 long, sweaty minutes to reach Terry's repair shop. I park in back and find him inside. I tell Terry I was just hanging out with Billy. We catch up a little as we walk to the car.

Looking at the damage, he says, "When do you need it?"

"In a couple of days, tops. It's my brother's, so it's got to look new."

"Quick job'll cost a little more, but we can do it."

The price he quotes makes me dizzy, but I'm relieved he doesn't ask any questions. We shake hands to seal the deal.

Heading home, I realize I'm going to have to scrape together every cent I have in the world, plus more. Yet I feel everything worked out right. Everyone got what they deserved, including me.

May 1964

Leaning across the table in Junior's restaurant, Andy Weiss tells me, "I just found out that tomorrow the chaplain of West Point is coming to give a speech to students who are in the Army's ROTC program. The administration is trying to keep it hush-hush. They don't want us finding out and disrupting his pious pep talk."

"Wait," I say, "I thought when they bring in an outside speaker, it's open to all students."

"You're right. If we show up, they can't keep us out. But show up to do what?"

"Let's go Socratic. Let's ask the chaplain questions he's not used to getting. Like Jesus said, 'Blessed is the peacemaker.' How does he square that with being on the side of our government's war makers?"

"Or does he actually tell cadets that if they napalm innocent women and children, God's still gonna be OK with them getting into heaven?"

"Should we try to get our people together tonight and plan this out?"

"Not tonight, I have something important going on. Hey, how would you like to see Pete Seeger and Odetta singing together for free?" Andy asks.

"Sure. Where?"

"Brooklyn CORE's starting something new. There's this big kick-off at the Siloam Presbyterian Church in Bed-Stuy."

"I'm down."

Meeting in the evening; we take the subway to Franklin Avenue. With our eyes scanning the streets for trouble, we walk quickly past abandoned and dilapidated buildings to get to the church.

Although there are seats available downstairs, Andy leads me upstairs where we sit in the front row of the balcony. Leaning over the railing, my political friend scans the crowd.

"Seeger and Odetta sure can fill seats," he says.

"Looking for anyone in particular?"

"Undercover fuzz. The police department's Red Squad usually sends a plainclothes cop to spy on us."

"Here?"

"Of course, here. If Seeger's playing and the head of CORE is speaking, you can bet rats are listening. In Mississippi, the folks who trained us said we should look for people who almost fit in."

Reverend Milton Galamison steps to the pulpit. "Tonight at Siloam exciting things are happening. Some people call me a pain in the . . . you-know-what, because of my civil rights work. They charge me with wanting to be my brother's keeper. I plead guilty. Our church pleads guilty. We are our brother's keeper, our sister's keeper too, because that is what Jesus Christ, our Lord, commands us to be."

"Amen."

"Tonight we'll hear from our true representatives—Major Owens, the leader of the Brooklyn chapter of the Congress of Racial Equality, and Bayard Rustin, one of Dr. King's trusted advisers. Brother Pete Seeger and Sister Odetta have kindly offered to entertain us."

First up, Bayard Rustin, a prince of a man—dignified and articulate—delivers an impassioned speech on how the civil rights movement is expanding its scope.

"We must confront economic inequality because it is the root cause of the poverty and problems we see around us," Rustin says. "Without good jobs and a decent place to live, you can't have real freedom."

Shouts of "Right on, brother" echo through the church.

"Now please welcome two true friends. They sang with us at the March on Washington, they sang with the Freedom Riders in Alabama, and tonight in this blessed sanctuary, they're singing songs of freedom and justice. Pete Seeger and Odetta."

Pete, playing his banjo, and Odetta, strumming a guitar, walk to the front of the pulpit and start singing, "If You Miss Me at The Back of the Bus." The audience claps and sings along.

"Let's go downstairs and take a look around," Andy says.

Moving down the side aisle, I study the crowd, thinking "almost fit in." In the fifth row, there's this white guy, thirtyish, wearing a new jean jacket. Instead of singing along, he's looking around, taking things in.

Is this a little rat? I point him out to Andy who nods. "I get the same vibe. Let's keep an eye on him."

After a rousing set, Seeger says, "Odetta and I raise our voices high in support of Brooklyn CORE. They know that real freedom means good schools, good jobs, and honest public officials. Please give Major Owens your full attention."

Cheers and foot stomping welcome Owens, dressed in a business suit, to the pulpit. His determined voice booms through the church. "Brooklyn CORE has a message to send to this city's leaders about freedom and peace. Freedom means holding a decent job so you can give your children everything they deserve. Peace means having a safe place to live. Right here in Brooklyn, CORE organized a rent strike. The most successful one this town's ever seen. Over a hundred buildings joined up and together, with one voice, we declared, 'No more broken furnaces, no more leaky roofs, no more rats and roaches. We demand safe and secure places to live.' As you all know, as everyone knows, we won that strike. We put the city's powerbrokers and landlords on notice."

"That's the truth, brother."

"Tonight, I'm here to tell you about a new, bold undertaking called the Brooklyn Freedom Democratic Movement. We're challenging the Democratic machine. It's a mighty hungry machine—takes our votes and gives us nothing in return. It's time our representatives represent the people, not the landlords and profiteers. So right here, right now, I am announcing my candidacy for the office of City Council from my neighborhood, your neighborhood, Bedford-Stuyvesant."

The crowd stands *en masse* cheering and applauding his announcement.

A young woman, with a close-cropped Afro, bracelets ringing her arms, and robed in a red, black, and green dashiki, takes the mic. "Our next councilman—Major Owens of the Brooklyn Freedom Democratic Movement. BFDM members are circulating donation buckets. Fill them high with your contributions. Sign-up sheets are out there too. Help us elect Major Owens, the people's candidate."

"I'm signing up," I say. "Brooklyn needs to get its shit together. How about you?"

"Already have," Andy says with a grin. "I'm the BFDM weekend office manager."

People are leaving. So is the rat. We tail him, keeping our distance. Going a block, he lights a cigarette, and we stop and pretend to talk. A black guy in penny loafers, green chinos, and a white tennis shirt joins him and they climb into a black '64 Plymouth.

"How come all unmarked police cars are always the same—black Furys?" I ask.

"Because they think everyone's stupid. Remember those bastards. Two of them here means CORE's got them scared."

"Seeger and Odetta are incredible. They fill me with hope."

"It was a great night, but seeing these two dicks means the party bosses are really threatened by what's happening. Things could get heavy. Mark, this is how the game is played. The pigs can go outside the law, break all the rules—infiltrate the movement, wiretap our phones, set us up for busts—while we have to make damned sure every single thing we do is legit. Break one law and they'll break us."

May 1965

PARKEE

Summer starts in a storm of failure. In a single week, I get tossed out of Baruch College and dumped by my girlfriend Barb who's on the Dean's List at Hunter College. So when the Parks Department responds to my employment application by offering me a summer job as a Seasonal Recreational Specialist, a parkee, I'm elated.

The one-day training session begins with Mr. Smith, our athletically-built district supervisor, distributing packets of forms and information. Explaining the proper way to fill out time cards, he says, "Under no circumstances is anyone to punch anyone else's time card. Understand?"

Accident and Incident Reports are reviewed, but we're advised, "Good recreational specialists have no need of such forms."

Included in the packets are mimeographed sheets about recreational activities, including games like badminton that have absolutely no chance of being played at any self-respecting Brooklyn playground.

A fellow parkee raises his hand. "How do we get things like basketballs?"

Nodding, Smith directs us to the Equipment Request Form. "The only time you are to fill this out is *after* you have received your equipment."

The questioner starts to respond, then grins and says, "Oh, I get it, thanks."

We all receive two official, blue and orange NYC Parks Department T-shirts. Our training's done.

The next morning, Mr. Smith drives several of us to Bushwick—one dangerous neighborhood. When he turns right onto Ellery Street, I gulp. The Ellery Street Bops are Brooklyn's toughest Puerto Rican gang. Pulling up to the playground, he looks at his clipboard, and says, "Berger, you're home."

Going into the park house, Mr. Smith introduces me to Walter Washington, the maintenance man, who looks like a bowling ball with legs. We shake hands.

After Smith drives off, Washington says, "Welcome to our little house. I best tell you about this park."

"I heard about the Ellery Street Bops. Word is they're bad news."

"They can be mean motherfuckers. Have to be 'cause Bushwick's mostly colored and a lot of my people don't like all the PRs who be moving in. Me? I'm not into that. I go to church. The Bops watch out for their own and they don't take no shit from nobody."

"How do I ID one?"

"Easy. 'Stead of belts, they tie together a couple of bandanas. Now the department thinks this is their park. T'ain't. Only body that runs this place is the Bops. They want to drink here, play drums, make out, then they do. Want to rumble, then they do. Dig?"

"I dig."

Looking out the window, he nods toward some benches opposite us. "See that hole in the fence behind that bench? That's the easiest way to the subway. See that tall, skinny cat playing handball?"

I look across the playground to the handball courts and spot a bare-chested cat with long, black hair.

"That there's Lopez, their leader. Don't sweat Smith, sweat Lopez."

I spend the bulk of the day organizing things in the storage closet which has Nok Hockey pucks and sticks, but no boards. Taking a tour of the playground, I smile at the little kids and watch a ferocious game of handball.

Near quitting time, Walter and I are back in the park house. Four Bops sit facing us on the top slat of a bench, Mongo Santamaria blares from their big portable radio.

When Lopez joins them, Washington says, "I got to leave early today. Berger, punch me out." I nod, he splits.

Lopez opens a bag and passes around a bottle of wine. Next, he brings out a saw and starts cutting the top slat of the bench next to theirs into one-foot pieces. Taking a turn, another gang member starts on the second slat. In no time there's a pile of pieces in front of them.

Standing back from the park house window, so they can't see me, I'm transfixed. *What now?*

Lopez takes a drag of his cigarette, blows smoke rings, and surveys his realm. Then he picks up a piece of wood and hurls it against the metal park house door. The others say something, laugh and do the same. Inside the house, it sounds like a thunderstorm.

It's five o'clock, quitting time, but what am I going to do? I can't stay in here. It's not safe—there's no phone, no back way out. I picture them setting the wood on fire.

What'd Washington say? This is their park. If they want to chop benches up, then they do. If they want to jump me, then they do. Pure and simple.

Taking a deep breath, I know what I have to do. I leave the building, but instead of going out the main entrance, I head directly toward where they're sitting. Stepping onto the seat of the now backless bench, I hesitate a moment before going through the hole in the fence.

Glancing at Lopez, I go, "Later."

His crew tenses. He looks straight ahead. "Mañana."

A piece of wood hits the ground behind me, but I keep walking. The handball players watch as I split.

Next morning, Washington cleans up the mess. Mr. Smith arrives with four basketballs, a Nok Hockey set and some other things. Thanking him, I sign the Equipment Received Form and use it to fill out the Equipment Request Form, proving the Park Department always delivers. The Incident Reports sit untouched.

I bring one of the basketballs out to the court. Everyone comes over, sides are picked.

"*Bueno, hombre,*" a Bop says.

At five o'clock, I head out through the fence. Lopez is playing handball. He ignores me. The only thing Lopez and his boys demand is respect. I can respect that. Today we're cool.

July 1964

SLUGS

Henry's yellow and red dashiki stands out against the dark green entrance of the Paradox, the vegetarian restaurant on Seventh Street between First and Second Avenue in the East Village. We're grabbing a bite before heading a few blocks over to catch some jazz.

As we sit, I notice my pal is carrying a case.

"Henry, what's that?" I ask.

"Soprano sax. Just got it," he replies.

"Slugs tonight, too cool. I'm excited."

"Me too. Don't wanna miss Archie Shepp." Looking serious, he says, "Mark, I'm not Henry Harrison anymore. I'm Kareem Malik?"

"Wha? You go underground?" I ask in a friendly, mocking way.

"No, I've become a Muslim."

"A Muslim? I thought Muslims ain't supposed to be seen dead with white folks, let alone Jews."

"I'm not a Black Muslim. Elijah Mohammad uses the Koran to divide people. Real followers of Islam want to unite people."

I nod, he continues, "My big cousin did some time upstate. Went in as James, came out as Abdul, a changed man. He accepted Allah and, for the first time in his life, he's doing what a man should do: taking care of himself, his family, working steady, no more jitterbuggin'. He took me to his mosque and now I'm Kareem Malik. This is for real."

"Hey, if it makes you feel good and we can still be friends, I got no problem calling you Kareem. You're not quitting college, are you?"

"What and break my mama's heart? I got to hit the books harder 'cause I'll need a good job if I'm gonna live a righteous life."

"Archie Shepp better be righteous too 'cause Slugs is past Avenue B, deep in Alphabet City."

"We best keep our eyes open. Junkies don't get us, the winos will."

"Slugs is the home of free jazz." I go, "Sun Ra and Ornette Coleman gig there. Let's eat up and go."

Once we cross Avenue A, people move purposefully down the streets. No stopping and hanging out here. Turning the corner of Third and Avenue B, we hear jazz blasting. Down a couple of steps, we enter a long thin room with posters on the walls and sawdust on the floor. The crowd is a cool mix of whites, blacks and Puerto Ricans. Race doesn't matter here, hipness does and with Kareem's Afro and my shoulder-length hair we fit right in.

We grab a table to the right of the stage. Next to us, this thirtyish, academic-looking man, wearing horn-rimmed glasses and a tweed sports jacket, is explaining group improvisation to his young, mini-skirted date who could be one of his students.

"Started with Bird, Dizzy, Trane, very talented improvisers," he says. "And then Ornette Coleman came up with the idea of group improvisation. When it's works, it takes you to another realm, a cosmic space."

"Yeah, like acid," the chick says.

Before he can respond, the emcee introduces Archie Shepp and his quintet.

Dressed in a blue dashiki, the leader steps to the mic. I recognize Ed Blackwell, Ornette's powerhouse drummer. On the downbeat, they blast off. Fusillades of sound—strident, discordant, soaring—strafe the room, ricocheting off everything. Shepp's tenor is raw and unrelenting. Blackwell's drumming is explosive. This music takes no prisoners. Dig it or get lost.

I feel like diving under the table. Kareem's listening intently.

After playing for almost an hour, Blackwell signals that he is having trouble with his drums, so the band slows to a halt. As he fixes his kit, I lean across the table, "This stuff is overpowering."

"Man, it's the future, right here and now. Stay with it, you'll dig it."

"Yeah, I'm hip. I'll be deaf before I'm 25."

"This next piece will close out the set," says the bandleader. "Thanks for coming out tonight"

Across from me, Kareem opens his instrument case, assembles his soprano sax and blows into it a couple of times. When the band starts up, Kareem strides onto the bandstand and joins in. Shepp says something to him, Kareem says something back, and, to my amazement, they slap each other five. Several minutes in, Archie points to my friend who steps forward and starts wailing.

Announcing the band members to the cheering crowd, Archie Shepp says, "Our brother, Kareem Malik, joined us on soprano tonight. Let's have a hand for him." More cheers.

On the street, my friend is walking on air.

"Kareem, how many lessons have you had?"

"None. Well, this is my first."

I feel like saying, this proves it. No training is no hindrance to performing free jazz, but I keep my lips zipped.

"Why didn't you tell me you know Archie Shepp?"

"I don't, at least I didn't before I got on the bandstand."

"Bro, you mean you just walked up there and jammed with those cats. Weren't you scared?"

"I just knew I could do it. Thanks be to Allah."

"I hope you know you'll have to stay friends with me forever because I'm your only witness. 'I was there the night Kareem Malik, an upstart, upstaged Archie Shepp.' Man, oh, man."

"Have to stay friends with you? What a price to pay."

Pushing each other and laughing, we stride to the subway, feeling like members of the hip elite.

May 1968

BOOM

Tink slides glasses of orange soda laced with amphetamine around the table to Spider, Lionel, Zooby, and me. Toasting each other, we down the contents as Zooby intones "*l'chaim*." To life.

In this crazy apartment on the top floor of a tenement in Midwood, I finally feel like I belong. I dig these cats because we're trying to figure out how life works and where we fit in. To get answers, we're delving into psychology, religion, and science, listening to music from everywhere, and experimenting with better living through chemistry. Often we stay up and rap the whole night long.

Three months ago, on my first acid trip, I could feel how everything was connected to everything else. The trees and plants seemed sentient, even the furniture emanated energy. Later, when I told Zooby, he said, "Just what I need, a vibrating couch." But still, I understood the world in a whole new way.

Looking around the table at my fellow psychic explorers, I say, "Spider challenged me to read some of Freud's books and so I did. Here's some of what I found out. Freud sees through a lot of crap, like he believes that our dreams, the silly mistakes we make, have meaning. But that meaning is hidden from us, buried in our unconscious. And because of that, people never get hip to themselves."

"Just playing games instead of being real," goes Spider. "Like what Eric Berne says in *Games People Play*."

"Check this out," chimes in Zooby. "In *Siddhartha*, Hermann Hesse's book, Siddhartha goes through all this shit. Then he gets into meditation and realizes, 'Yeah, life's a game, but to win it, you got to quit it.' So he drops out and becomes enlightened. Sounds like a plan to me."

"Anyone hear *Nowhere Man*, the new Beatles song?" Lionel asks.

We ignore him and move on.

Tink's up next. He holds up a ballpoint pen and clicks it. "I was thinking what else has a point. Umbrellas, they have points too? So what could I do if I turned an umbrella into a ballpoint pen? Let's say, I stick a plunger and spring in the point, and connect it to a tube. Now here's the good part," he pauses to laugh, "instead of ink coming out, it's pot seeds. OK? So on a rainy day, we all go into Prospect Park and roam around using these umbrellas like canes, and each time we push the handle, a seed gets planted. Come spring, we've turned the park into a pot plantation—reefer growing everywhere, free for the taking."

The laughter rises from the table, and we each slap him five. Zooby says, "That's a beautiful idea. We'll have to change the sign that says 'Welcome to Prospect Park' to 'Welcome to Pot Park.'"

A joint gets passed around. Tink puts on a record of John Cage talking. The avant-garde composer says, "Everything is music, life is music."

"Now that's a deep thought," says Lionel.

Spider says he has something important to discuss, but it's approaching dawn, and we're all talked out. By now we're sitting on the floor. We wrap ourselves in our coats and doze off.

Awake around 10, we head down the street to a luncheonette. On the way, I say to Spider, "Lionel's our Nowhere Man. Let's lose him."

Spider waves off my suggestion.

After we all order French toast and coffee, Spider looks around, leans in, and talks just above a whisper. "We all know LSD's going to change everything, but the Man knows it too. That's why good acid's getting harder to score and getting the chemicals so we can make it ourselves is impossible."

"Believe me, we tried. We need ergotamine," says Tink. "It's supposed to be legal, but no chemical supply house will sell it to regular people like us."

"Me and the Tink have been doing research," says Spider. "We found something new. It's called DMT, dimethyltryptamine."

"It's got 'trip' right in its name," says Lionel.

Tink shushes him. "Let's go back to my place and we'll tell you more."

We pony up the money for the bill and march back to his pad.

"On Monday Lionel drove us up to Edmund Scientific, outside of Buffalo, and we copped the basic chemicals," Spider says.

"Lionel fronted the money. We plunked it down and walked out with the goodies," Tink cackles.

"We turned out a small batch for us all to try. If it's the real thing, then we'll go into production."

"Whoa," I say. "What's it do?"

"First off, it's not a pill," replies Spider. "You take a toke and boom. It hits like a locomotive."

"Drops you right in the middle of a heavy-duty acid trip." Tink goes. "Take a hit and hit the floor."

"But dig this, it only lasts 10 minutes," says Spider.

"Instead of coffee breaks, people gonna be taking DMT breaks," Lionel adds.

Spider unwraps a piece of tin foil, showing us a congealed substance, the size of a walnut with the odor of ether.

Lionel takes out a hash pipe.

Tink says, "Everyone ready?"

We sit in a circle on the floor and nod yes.

With Spider filling the pipe and Tink lighting it, it goes from Lionel to Zooby to me and back to the chemists.

Outside the window is a big oak tree. I tell myself I might be able to stay grounded by staring at the branches. But in a second it all disappears, gone, replaced by swirls of colors. Loud sounds like crashing garbage cans fill my ears. I lie back and am engulfed by psychedelic hallucinations. Sometimes they're coming at me, sometimes there's no me, I'm part of it. In a moment of clarity, I reassure myself it lasts only a few minutes. A hysterical howl sounds in my head and I know that in this inner space ten minutes doesn't exist. There is no time here. There's only now.

The swirling ebbs. Shapes regain their natural outline. I hear a toilet flushing. Opening my eyes, I see everyone is smiling at me.

"Man, you were gone the longest," says Lionel.

"Time, time just disappeared," I say.

"Was I spaced out," says Zooby.

"I could hear my brain cells exploding," says Lionel.

We sit silently taking in what just went down.

"Are we good to go?" asks Spider.

"Yeah, we're good," we say.

A half hour later, Zooby and I take the bus to the Brooklyn Botanic Garden, our sanctuary.

It's February. The paths are glazed with ice. Making a beeline to a favorite winter place, we pass through the heat and humidity of the tropical greenhouse and open a door to a large rectangular room that's sunlit, cool and quiet. Arranged on tables around its periphery are bonsai trees—miniature Japanese maples, Chinese junipers, and Blue Atlas cedars, some centuries old.

Sitting down, we just breathe in and out for a while taking in the bonsais' humble majesty.

Turning to my best friend, I ask, "Did we just become guinea pigs?"

"Uh-uh. We're astronauts of inner space, and we're on a new mission."

February 1966

THE TEAM

"You're killing Mom and Dad," my brother Paul tells me on the phone.

"We're driving each other nuts. I gotta move out. It's past time."

"There are construction jobs down here. You interested?"

"Yeah. What's Lois say?"

"You're my brother, so it's my call, but she definitely wants our kids to have grandparents."

Two weeks later, I'm in the backseat of their Volvo heading to Arlington, Virginia, just outside of DC, where Paul is in George Washington Law School and his wife, Lois, teaches high school English.

Paul has seen a "help wanted" sign in the window of a nearby home improvement company called "Gud-z-Nu Construction." When I tell the office manager, who's named Hollis, that I worked construction in Brooklyn, he hires me on the spot. The following day, he drives me in a pickup to a light blue, suburban house with a steep backyard.

"Owners want this leveled for a patio," he says pointing to a slanting backyard about 20-feet square.

"Where's the backhoe?" I ask.

"Ain't none. Wheelbarrow, shovel, and pick's all you need."

Drenched in sweat, I work steadily all day and make slow, hard progress.

Driving me back to the office, Hollis says, "That's all I got this week."

"Friday pay day?"

"Boss is out of town. Call me on Monday."

I'm no fool, so I start looking for another gig. Borrowing my brother's car, I drive around to construction sites. By Thursday, I have a lead on one at a new garden apartment development.

At exactly ten o'clock, I enter the construction office, where there's this guy, about 50 and bald, sitting at a desk.

"Hi, I'm Mark Berger and I'm looking for work. Called yesterday and they told me to come see the foreman today at ten."

"That'd be me," the man says, looking me over. "Name's Phillips, but everyone calls me Preacher. Show up tomorrow, with a hammer, 7:30 sharp and we'll give you a try."

Next morning, Preacher calls to a guy carrying a stack of 2 by 4's on his shoulder. "Ronnie, take this man over to Tracy. He's your new helper."

Walking a diagonal across the site, Ronnie asks, "Where you from?"

"Brooklyn. Brooklyn, New York."

"Me-oh-my. West Virginia's my home."

We climb two flights of stairs to a large deck. Hammers are clanking. On a ladder is this very tall, sinewy carpenter.

"What took you so long?" he asks Ronnie.

"Preacher told me to bring you the new helper. He's from Brooklyn."

"Brooklyn?" says the carpenter, "Guy I was in the Army with came from there—Melvin Snyder. Ya know him?"

" 'Fraid not."

"Well, no matter. You're in Dixie now, son," Tracy says, extending his hand.

Each morning at seven, our hammers start their thumping, we take a half hour for lunch and continue until quitting time. We're the framing crew—four carpenters and two helpers. Using blueprints, we build the walls and partitions of one apartment and move on to the next, one floor at a time, one building at a time. Tracy is powerful, efficient, and accurate. He can drive in a 20-pound box of nails in a day. Once a stud, joist, or sheet of plywood is set in place, Ronnie and I pound in additional nails to secure it.

Kelly, a carpenter out of Kentucky, starts calling me "New York" and it sticks. It's the only nickname I've ever had. I do my best to earn it by working hard and, on occasion, being a wiseass. We're a team. Our uniform: sunburnt torsos, baseball caps, jeans, steel-toed boots, nailing aprons with hammers and tape measures attached. Within a week, I'm in cadence with the others. Sometimes we go for hours without talking—each guy carrying his weight, doing his job. We're a machine of grace and power.

Each day as we're packing up, I walk around and think with pride, we're building homes for families.

One day, a pallet of floorboards comes apart and I'm sent to hand load them onto the forklift. As I do, Elvin, the obese, unshaven operator starts mouthing off to me about the company.

"Jews. Jews own this. But you ever see them here? Uh-uh. Preacher's their slave driver and we're the slaves."

"That so?"

"The Jews make the money and we bust our asses."

"That so?"

"Ever notice when one Jew moves into a place, the others set him up in business. Plain folks ain't got no chance."

"Hey, Elvin, is it true what I hear, that you make twice what I make?" I ask.

"Could be, why?"

"Well, here I am sweating my ass off loading these boards while you're sitting up there, yakking away, making two dollars for every one I make. Here's the thing: I'm Jewish. Nobody ever saved me from hard work. I'm just like you, a working man."

Two days later, Preacher takes me off the framing crew and reassigns me to the milling shop where I work with a taciturn carpenter named Raoul. Ronnie tells me my new job's a cinch, but for me, it hurts.

Discussing it later with Paul and Lois they point out that Elvin might have told Preacher and my crewmates about my religion and that's what got me kicked off the team.

"Could that really be true? Could being Jewish count more than doing a good job?"

They both nod.

"If it is, it's too depressing for words."

August 1966

SATURDAY NIGHT SPECIAL

"I don't have much time," I mutter to myself as I unlock the door to my apartment in a rundown building on Duffield Street, right across Flatbush Avenue from my college, Long Island University. Unpacking a buttered bagel and a cup of coffee on the wire-spool table, I turn on the light and plop down on a couch that Zooby and I found two weeks ago and dragged back here. Natasha, a friend of ours, dressed it up with a couple of colorful cushions and a red paisley bedspread.

Bone-tired from working the graveyard shift at a technical printing company, I only have 20 minutes to eat and get to my nine o'clock class. With a regular gig and a college loan, I can afford rent and food, which makes me a rarity among my friends. Often there's someone crashing at my place, but not this morning.

My big idea was to read *Siddhartha* and *The Magic Mountain* in German, but learning that language is a motherfucker. Spoken it sounds like someone's choking and written is even crazier. I take out my *Beginning German* workbook, struggle to do my assignment and close the book in frustration.

As I sip the coffee, a glint of something catches my eye. Packing up my green book bag the glint becomes an uneasy feeling. What's that sticking out of the couch? Hastily digging into the cushions, my hand grasps something cold. I find myself holding a small revolver with the barrel pointing right at me.

"Easy does it," I say out loud.

Checking the safety, the way my pal Billy once showed me, I'm relieved that it's on. Turning the gun over in my hand, I admire its sleek, black, steel body and snub nose.

The newspapers dub these .22 caliber revolvers Saturday Night Specials. They're built for two things—causing damage and creating mayhem. Lots of little hard guys feel like big tough men with one of these in their waistband.

My hands tremble as I open the chamber. Out fall three bullets. Where did this gun come from? Whose is it? How did it end up here in my couch? No time to fathom an explanation. Got to go to class. Can I afford another cut? No, I cannot.

I've got to stash the piece somewhere. Moving quickly, I wrap the gun and bullets in paper towels and place them in the large garbage bag in the kitchen, the one that always needs to go out. By the cellar stairs, I open one of the building's metal trash cans. Repositioning my neighbors' junk, I place mine at the bottom. I'm about to go when I realize I better check the hallway sign to see if today's the garbage pickup day. It's not. For now, it's in a safe place.

The sky's full of rain clouds. Flatbush Avenue's full of speeding cars. As I cross the street midblock, a horn honks at me. I glare at the driver and keep on jaywalking.

Professor Engel, my language teacher, begins each class by addressing us in basic conversational German.

She asks me, "*Wie geht es Ihnen heute?*" How are you today?

I want to say "Not so good because someone may want to blow my brains out," but instead I grumble, "*Gut danke*," Good, thank you, and slink way down in my chair.

After that, she leaves me alone.

Walking back home, I admit to myself that letting people I don't know stay at my pad may seem cool, but in reality it's an awful, terrible idea. The gun proves it. I wonder what's going to happen when the asshole who left it comes back to get it.

September 1966

GONE

Sunday night, I'm feeling pretty good as I dress for my job. No one shot me this weekend. I still have the pistol I found on Friday. I waited and worried but no one came to claim it.

After class, I had taken it from the garbage can and stashed it in a Brillo box under the kitchen sink. As I'm about to go out the door, I decide to say goodnight to the snub-nosed .22. Taking out the box, I see the pads are askew. I dig to the bottom. Nothing. The gun's gone.

Does it possess some perverse magic that allows it to appear and disappear at will? Uh-uh, someone took it. I was here all weekend and nothing happened. No time to cogitate, I've got to go. On the subway, it hits me. Hank and Jay came by last night and stayed over. I was asleep when they split to return to college in Buffalo.

Used to be Hank and me were best buddies. But now things have changed. He hangs out with this guy, Jay, who I know from Ocean Parkway. Zooby calls him the Troll. Hank's always going on about what he and Jay are doing—like writing for the *Spectrum*, the campus newspaper, getting involved in student protests and acting like Buffalo is this hip place when it's clearly not.

I picture last night. Hank passes around a bottle of burgundy. I do the same with a joint.

Hank starts reminiscing. "Remember that time we were at Al's place, way uptown, 122nd Street, totally stoned, listening to "Lady in Satin" with Antonio, the building super, and his wife, Alba?"

"And Alba sang just like Lady Day."

"Man, she nailed 'But Beautiful.'"

"Hey, remember when that barkeep on Church Avenue refused to serve us 'cause we had long hair?" I ask.

Hank turns to Jay. "So we stop a cop and tell him the bartender's violating the new Civil Rights Act and the fuzz goes, 'That law's only for the South.'"

"What an idiot," I say and we both laugh.

Jay listens in stony silence. To impress or scare him—who knows why?—I tell them about the pistol and take it out to show it off. Talk about stupid.

When I get a break at work, I call Hank from a pay phone. "Sorry I'm calling so late, but I gotta know if you have *that something* I showed you."

"Not me. What about your people?"

"Nah, you're the only ones I showed it to. Do me a solid, ask Jay?"

Hank mumbles something to Jay and I hear him answer, "Yeah, I got it. He said he didn't want it, so I'm doing him a favor."

"Put him on the line."

"What's up?"

"Listen, you fuckin' troll. I said I wasn't sure what to do with it, not 'Jay take it.' What if its owner shows up and doesn't want to take no for an answer? And besides, why in a million years would I give it to you?"

Hank gets back on, "What's the big deal?"

"If your weirdo pal shoots someone, shoots himself, or get busted showing it off, it'll all land in my fuckin' lap. So, listen to me and do what I say. Tell Jay that you're holding it now. I'll be up next weekend to get it."

Friday evening, I fly Mohawk Airlines to Buffalo and go straight to the *Spectrum* office. Hank and Jay are the only ones there. Barely saying hello, Hank hands me a manila envelope. Checking the contents, I slide it in my book bag, say *ciao* and head out the door. Jay's glowering at me, but who really cares.

"Where you staying?" Hank asks.

"Someplace safe."

Once off campus, I make a beeline for Bitterman's, a working man's bar with a jukebox loaded with Sinatra, Ella and Harry James. Over a boilermaker, I think, *I've got what I came for, now what am I going to do with it?*

Leaving the bar, I walk a couple of blocks, until I'm all alone. Opening the envelope, I look inside. Guns, all they cause are trouble. I slide the envelope down a sewer. Walking back to the main drag, I get a cab to the bus station where a Greyhound is leaving at midnight. Taking a seat, I think about how Hank and I are barely friends anymore, we're traveling different roads. As the bus charges down the Thruway, I count up my losses.

October 1966

REVOLTING

"Mr. Berger, please, take a seat," Mr. O'Brien says as he points to a chair directly in front of his desk.

"Yes, sir."

O'Brien is my height with a beer-belly, large hands, a bulbous nose, and protruding ears that frame his short gray hair. Word is he served in the Marines and was an FBI agent. Here at Volt Tech, he's head of security. Since I work the graveyard shift, this is our first meeting.

"Mr. Berger, you understand, part of my job is to meet with employees who are leaving the company?"

"Yes."

"Our contract with the Department of Defense mandates that employees, such as yourself, having Secret Clearance, must participate in an exit interview. Are you familiar with the Espionage Act?"

"I think they mentioned it when I was hired."

"The Espionage Act specifies that any employee who shares information about classified documents or provides copies of classified documents to anyone outside this company is engaging in espionage. You are aware of this, correct?"

"I know that. What's it got to do with me?"

"Maybe nothing, maybe everything. Mr. Berger, why you are resigning your position?"

"I've been working the graveyard shift and attending college classes full time and I just can't keep it up. I can't sleep, I'm exhausted all the time."

He leans in so he can look me in the eye. "Have you shared any information or documents with anyone outside this firm—a girlfriend, a friend, a college acquaintance?"

Unable to control myself, I smirk. "I'm sorry, but I find your question kind of funny. How to say this? No one I know has the slightest interest in what work I do."

"Mr. Berger, do you support the war America is fighting in Southeast Asia?"

"Am I for the Vietnam War?"

"Companies are like small towns. People talk. It's come to my attention that you're against the war. Is that correct?"

"Mr. O'Brien, I'm deeply troubled by it. I think it's wrong, maybe immoral."

"Immoral? Who told you the war's immoral?"

"You read the papers, see it on TV. I wanted to find out more so I've read *Street without Joy* and some other stuff. I don't think we should be there. Vietnam belongs to the Vietnamese, like the U.S. belongs to us."

"These things you read, who told you about them? What antiwar meetings have you been attending?"

"Meetings? Who's got time for meetings? Oh, I get it, you mean like meeting meetings, like Commie meetings. I'd never go to one of those. Russia and China make me sick. They're police states."

"Mr. Berger, it might surprise you to know that many groups that say they're antiwar are actually Communist-front organizations. They're experts at taking unsuspecting young people and selling them the Red Line. What have they been feeding you?"

"I don't join groups. I try to figure things out for myself."

"I'm trying to help you to remember who gave you this idea that the war is immoral—a friend, maybe, a professor?"

"Mr. O'Brien, you're making me nervous again. I'm telling you the truth, but you're not hearing me."

"Our enemies watch places like Volt Tech hoping to befriend young workers. I've seen it time and again. I served in the FBI. I know things you don't. There are people whose goal is to have our young people hate their own country and the first thing they do is instill the idea that America is immoral."

O'Brien continues, "We're in Vietnam to stop the Commies from expanding their control. If we pull out of that

God-forsaken place, then in no time all of Asia will fall under Communist domination."

"Mr. O'Brien, I never see a complete document, I only work on pieces. I'm not an engineer, I'm a proofreader. My job is to make sure that whatever the tech writer writes, the copy setter sets. Recently I started thinking that, maybe, in some small way, my work here was supporting this war and that, maybe, I was helping to kill people. That's when I stopped being able to sleep. Mr. O'Brien, I just can't work here anymore."

Holding up a paper, he says, "You have to sign this. It acknowledges what I told you about the Espionage Act."

"I understand, you're doing your job. You don't have to worry."

"Mr. Berger, I'm not worried. If you haven't told me the complete truth, you're the one who'd better worry. You are telling me the truth, aren't you?"

"Where do I sign?"

November 1966

SHRINK

On May Day, the letter I've been dreading from my draft board arrives ordering me to a pre-induction physical at Fort Hamilton. I've already been to an antiwar psychologist who wrote a letter saying I was mentally unfit for service, "This should get you in to see the Army psychiatrist," he said, "but you'll have to be convincing."

Ten days later, I report to the base and, along with a room full of other young men, go through the physical exams. Handing the psychologist's letter to a sergeant, I'm sent upstairs to the psychiatrist. Of the four others already there, only one seems loony. He's licking his fingers and talking to himself.

As I sit down, this tall, skinny, black cat sashays in wearing a fez, shades, a collarless jacket, harem pants, high-top sneakers, and lipstick, all the color of grape jelly.

He says, "I must warn them it's a serious violation of interstellar law for a cosmic being like myself to serve in another planet's army." Then he plops down on the floor right outside the shrink's door. All of us, except finger-licking-boy, are grinning. This cat's assertiveness kind of makes up for his lack of an authentic looking spacesuit.

Opening the door to his office to let out the person he just interviewed, the psychiatrist, in his thirties and dressed in civilian clothes, is startled when Purple Man just strides in declaring, "Interstellar beings first."

The guy who exits has a beard, long hair and a black leather jacket adorned with a button that reads, "Fuck You." I do a double take. It's my cousin Albert. We haven't seen each other in years.

I heard he had been living in Big Swede's East Village commune. They're the ones who opened the Psychedelicatessen, one of the city's first head shops. The police showed their appreciation by planting some dope in the store and, then, busting everyone for possession.

Albert looks as stoned as a Navaho shaman during a peyote ceremony. Getting his attention, I lead him to a corner.

"Albert, what're the odds?"

"It's Breezy. No one knows me as Albert."

"Breezy?"

"Breezy."

Nodding toward the psychiatrist's door, I ask, "How'd it go?"

"Shrink asks me, 'When's the last time you did drugs?' I say, 'We smoked hash coming over the bridge to get here.'

" 'When's the last time you did LSD?' I say, ''Round midnight. That's why I smoked the hash.' Laughing, he continues, 'Didn't want to be too spaced at the base.'

" 'Do you hear voices?' I tell him, 'All the time, don't you?' That was it. Nearly got freaked out when that purple cat strutted in, but like Swede says, 'We don't have to travel into space looking for intelligent life. ETs are already here.' " With that, my cousin waves his hand and splits.

Purple Man exits the office smiling. Two others come and go. These interviews are moving fast. I'll only have a couple of minutes to make my case. If I can't talk my way out, they'll send me to Vietnam where lifetimes can shrink down to the speed of a bullet.

"Berger."

It's show time. Although, I'm prepared for his questions, I can tell my answers aren't helping me get that psychological deferment. Finally, he asks: "Have you had any sexual relations with other males?"

Answering "yes" I've been told is an automatic 4F. So I surprise myself when I say, "No. I'm going to level with you. I'm here because I'm not crazy. The people who're really insane are the ones sending us to Vietnam."

"Would you have felt the same way about World War II?"

"That one we had to fight. Hitler had to be stopped. I would've enlisted. But this? These poor peasants have been defending their country against foreigners like us for like hundreds of years. All they want is their independence and to be left alone. This war's bullshit. It's a sham."

Looking at me sympathetically, he says, "I'm not for it either."

"Then how can you do this?"

"I tell myself I'm more understanding than other Army psychiatrists would be."

Gritting my teeth, I say, "You shrinks should reclassify our leaders as 4F. That way they won't be allowed to run the military. I don't want to kill for nothing. I don't want to die for nothing. Keep me out. I don't want any part of this insanity."

Folding his hands, he says, "My job's to determine if you're mentally ill. You're not."

There's nothing more to say.

Leaving, I feel righteous and distressed. I told the truth all right. But, now I'm one step closer to being drafted.

May 1966

CONTACT

In a small, smelly vestibule on Classon Avenue, we stomp the snow off our shoes and dust off our coats. Zooby says to Tink and me, "Where are we—Brooklyn or Alaska?"

"I can't believe we just trudged through a storm to get to Hammer's hovel," I say. "The radio show better be good 'cause this is totally nuts."

"Hamowitz ain't that bad," Tink says.

"The dude's a drag, always ranting about something," I go.

"Not about something," says Zooby, "about everything."

Misshapen and mismatched, Paul Hamowitz opens his apartment door. Seeing me, he says, "If you told me Berger was coming, I wudda said no."

"I dig you too," I say.

Looking behind me, Hammer continues, "And Zooby, too? Tink, have some mercy on me."

Tink laughs. "Let us in. The show's almost on."

"You should be honored," Zooby says. "This is the only place in the universe the three of us are appearing tonight."

"What's the big deal anyway?" our reluctant host asks.

"WBAI has this UFO show and tonight they got a NASA scientist who can prove he was abducted by aliens. The Pentagon's gonna fuckin' freak out when he dishes the truth."

"Far as I'm concerned, all three of you are space cadets," Hammer goes.

Instead of sitting on his dilapidated sofa, we drop our coats on the floor and sit on them.

Tuning the radio, Tink says, "When I was in the loony bin, I told the shrinks there had to be intelligent life somewhere in the universe since there sure ain't any on this fuckin' planet." He cackles at his own joke. "They thought I was stupid because once they call you crazy, automatically you're stupid. But I blew their minds—beat the shrinks at chess and taught myself chemistry, all while they had me doped up on zombie pills."

"Time for some head food," says Zooby, as he passes around a joint.

Taking a hit, I lean back and notice the cracks in the ceiling and the peeling paint on the walls. Talk about depressing. Talk about depressed—I got kicked out of college, so any day now the draft board's going to be knocking on my door. Plus my love life is lovelorn. I'm like a sinking ship. My life's a blues song. If it wasn't for bad luck, I wouldn't have no luck at all.

The announcer says due to technical difficulties tonight's scheduled show is postponed. Instead, they'll replay John Holt reading from his book *How Children Fail*.

"Think the Martians scooped the dude up again?" asks Zooby.

Tink's furious. "That proves it, the Man's scared. I bet they got that scientist locked up tight somewhere. I need some whiskey. Hammer, c'mon, take a walk to the liquor store. I'm buying."

"Long as these losers don't touch nothing."

"Don't worry," Zooby says, "We don't want any cooties. Anyway, who furnished this place, the sanitation department?"

"We're just going to listen to the radio," I say.

The door slams. Zooby closes his eyes and starts dozing off.

John Holt's angelic tenor wafts across the room. He describes how schools are places where children learn to fail. How real education happens when the child is the center of the classroom and not the teacher.

To make his argument, Holt tells classroom anecdotes that jolt me like a Muhammad Ali right jab. He's telling my story. I flash on all the trouble I've had with teachers over the years. He concludes by saying that we need new teachers and new approaches to replace the current moribund ones.

I'm overcome with sadness mixed with a strange stirring. Teaching? Should I become a teacher? I've never considered it, because I never liked school. But what Holt is saying is totally true, if I had had better teachers, my feelings would be different. Although I was smart, most teachers thought I was too smart, meaning I asked too many questions. But what if I became the kind of teacher that liked being asked questions? That respected and supported all the kids, even the ones who made it difficult? Maybe I could become one of those new teachers Holt is talking about. Make something of myself and contribute something of meaning to the world. Maybe. Maybe not.

The show ends, the door clicks open, snapping me out of my reverie. Tink and Hammer stumble in laughing and stoned. I give Zooby a nudge, we bundle up, mumble our goodbyes, and split.

Outside, my best friend asks: "You believe in flying saucers?"

"Not sure, but I feel like I've been contacted by the universe saying it has a mission for me."

"Do tell?"

"Not now, you wouldn't believe it anyway. How we getting home?"

"Ain't gonna be any buses. Maybe we can catch a dog sled."

The snow is still falling, the wind whips down the avenues, but inside I feel this warm spot. A little flame of hope just got kindled in me.

November 1964

"Did I tell you cats about the time in Mexico when Watts and I did mescaline together?" Peter Stafford asks us.

Spider raises his eyebrows to let Lionel and me know that Stafford's talking about the Alan Watts, the one who wrote *The Way of Zen*.

"Was that when you tripped in the desert?" Spider asks.

"No, that time I was with Tim Leary and Dick Alpert."

Stafford answers the phone. "Thanks for calling back. Leary's starting something big and he'd like you in on it. . . . Now's cool. Can I bring over a couple of young friends? . . . Thanks."

"Want to go to Allen Ginsberg's pad?" Stafford asks us.

"Sure," Spider says.

Peter tells us the cops are looking to bust Ginsberg—shut him up and shut him down. Anyone going to his place must be a hundred percent clean. Checking ourselves, Lionel takes a joint out of a pack of Camels and slides it on top of Stafford's Smith-Corona typewriter.

On the street, Lionel suggests we drive over in his car, but Stafford says it's lovely out, why not walk the six blocks. Glancing at our reflection in a store window, I see four characters. There's Peter, Ivy League, mid-30s, tall, blond, wearing a madras shirt and khaki shorts; Spider, rail thin, looking mod with hair down to his shoulders, a denim shirt, tight blue jeans over black boots; Lionel, stocky and unencumbered by style, with a white T-shirt and chinos; and me, dressed all in black. With Peter leading the way, we look like we're on a class trip from the Brooklyn School of Misfits.

Stafford and Spider walk ahead while Lionel and I hang back.

"Who's Allen Ginsberg?" Lionel asks.

"A poet, maybe America's best."

"Poetry's boring."

"I saw him live. It's mind-blowing, like going to dig Coltrane. Ginsberg's all about telling the truth about everything, himself included. He's a queer, a pothead, a pinko. His poetry doesn't just say it, it screams it. No apologies, no excuses."

"No wonder he's scared about getting busted."

"They'd lock him up in a minute."

At Seventh Street and Avenue B, we enter a nondescript, four-story apartment building. Climbing the stairs, Spider whispers, "Be cool."

As Peter rings the doorbell, I notice the name plate reads "A Ginsberg," no period.

The bald and bearded poet opens the door. Twinkling eyes enhance his warm smile. The apartment has the aroma of jasmine. We sit on red paisley cushions around a low table that displays a stick of burning incense, a small flower vase, and a photograph of Ginsberg, Peter Orlovsky and their guru.

Stafford begins, "Tim Leary is going to file official papers to establish a new religion which uses LSD as its sacrament. If the Navaho can legally use peyote in religious ceremonies, why can't we have a religion where acid is sacramental? This Friday's the first public meeting. He would be honored if you and Peter would attend."

"Starting a new religion? What an enterprising idea," says Ginsberg.

"If he wins in court, it would essentially legalize psychedelics," Stafford says.

"The last thing the religious pooh-bahs want their followers to find out is that they can commune with God on their own," Ginsberg goes.

Spider says, "That would be the end of the game for Western religion."

"Dr. Leary wants to liberate people," Ginsberg continues, "But lest we forget, in the land of the free, the free live in fear."

"What's the new religion called?" Lionel asks.

"League for Spiritual Discovery. Dig it?"

"Are your friends here invited?" Ginsberg asks.

"Um . . . Sure."

"Then let me find out who they are," says Ginsberg.

In a gentle way he asks me about myself.

"I'm Mark and I go to Long Island University."

"What're you studying?"

"You," I say with a grin. "Toby Olsen's my poetry teacher."

"Good poet."

Turning to Lionel, Ginsberg asks, "So what about you?"

"I work the counter in my old man's candy store in Flatbush, helping him out."

Spider and I exchange knowing glances—sure he helps out in front, 'cause his dad's running book in back.

"I bet you make delicious egg creams. You can't get good ones in Manhattan."

Spider's next. "They call me Spider. I'm a chemistry major. My friend and I are studying up on herbs because they're the basis of most medicines. We're thinking of starting an herbal products business."

"Amen. So how did you all meet my friend?" Ginsberg says pointing at Stafford.

"I read his book *LSD: The Problem-Solving Psychedelic*," says Spider. "He knows a lot about a lot I'm interested in."

"Spider looks me up in the phone book and calls me," Stafford says. "He says 'Let's talk.' I say, 'We're talking,' and he says, 'Phones aren't for talking.' So we meet. These guys are onto something."

"The three wise men, only they don't know it yet," the poet says cryptically.

As we get up to leave, Ginsberg gathers us to him. Looking from face to face, he intones, "Boys, be careful." Putting his hands together, he bows and says, "Peace."

After Stafford leaves us, Lionel goes, "Ginsberg's like my Uncle Harry. Always wanting to know everything about everybody."

"Yeah," says Spider, "only if your Uncle Harry wrote amazing poetry, smoked pot, meditated, and did it with men."

"I think we're down to two wise men," I say.

Getting into Lionel's Chevy Impala, Spider turns to me. "So, what do you think about Ginsberg?"

"Instead of ego-tripping like Stafford, Ginsberg wanted to find out about us. That's so cool. He's the real deal."

May 1966

Tennessee Reel

Walking into Barney's Luncheonette, I'm looking for my best friend Zooby. Sure enough, he's sitting in the back booth sipping a cup of coffee.

"Boy, am I happy you're here," I say. Getting a cup for myself along with two chocolate donuts, one for him, one for me, I slide into the booth.

"What's up?" Zooby asks.

"I had this weird thing happen to me when I was over at Red Marvin's."

"Word is he got in a little something."

Glancing around to make sure no one can hear us, I say, "More than a little, and it's Hawaiian. So, y'know, people are coming by to taste, talk, and score."

I take a sip and a bite. "Crazy Natasha was there and she's going on about how they used to smoke pot in the psych ward and I notice a couple of people nodding in agreement. Then Red Marvin says, 'In the pen, one joint cost a whole carton of cigarettes.' I see some others agreeing. So, going from face to face, I realize something: Every person there has either been in the loony bin or in the slammer, everyone, except me."

"Too much."

"Then a thought rockets into my mind: You're next. Guaranteed. Guaranteed? I think back to that .22 I found in my place and to all those other close calls, and Zooby, the universe is sending me a message. It's a serious warning. It's time for me to get far away from this scene."

"You moving to Queens?"

"Uh-uh, Tennessee, maybe. I called Roland, my friend in Baltimore, and told him about it. He said I should switch from Long Island University and go where he went—East Tennessee State University. Then he tells me about professors driving to school in farm trucks and corny stuff like that, and he had me laughing. But more than that, the school sounded nice and safe."

"Except one thing." Zooby says. "It's no accident our friends are our friends. You could go all the way there and end up hanging out with Tennessee Red Marvin."

~

Deciding to get more information, I call the East Tennessee State admissions office and they suggest I come take a look at the college and meet with the dean of admissions before submitting my application.

Three weeks later, I fly down to Johnson City, Tennessee. Through the admissions office, I've made arrangements to stay at a private home owned by a Mrs. Bishop. I arrive mid-afternoon and rent a car. Knocking on Mrs. Bishop's front door, her daughter, Leanne, who's at least three inches taller than me, answers. Since she's a student at ETSU, she insists on taking me on a brief campus tour and she brings along her little sister.

Compared to New York City standards, the campus is huge: plenty of trees and grass, crisscrossing paths, two- and three-story red brick buildings, and parking lots. The students look like, well, students, albeit very straight ones. Leanne takes me to the student union and shows me the white, columned administration building where I'll go for my interview in the morning.

Mrs. Bishop invites me to join her and her three daughters for dinner. Mindful of my manners, I set a personal record for saying please, thank you, and you're welcome. While answering their questions about New York, I notice my Brooklyn accent makes the girls giggle, but in a friendly way. These are good people: caring, sane, and safe. After they all go to bed, I sit on the porch contemplating my future.

In the morning at breakfast, dressed in a sport jacket, chinos, and a blue, button-down shirt, I touch on whether I will be accepted for admission or not. The girls wish me well. Mrs. Bishop says, "May the Lord's will be done." A no-lose proposition, if I've ever heard one.

As I leave, she hands me a pamphlet from her church. "If you come back, come on over."

Entering the administration building, I check myself out in the glass door. Before I left Brooklyn, I had my hair styled, and, although, it may be a tad long by Tennessee standards, it looks neat as does the rest of me. I've always done well on interviews, whether for jobs or for schools. I project confidence and sincerity, two personal characteristics that mean a lot to me and to interviewers.

Admissions Dean, Dr. Beardsley, is large and imposing in his brown, three-piece suit and bowtie. While most of his questions are predictable, I pause thoughtfully before replying to them.

He asks me, "Why have you chosen East Tennessee State University?"

I tell him, "My friend Roland Henderson graduated from here. He's always saying great things about the university. I want to be a teacher, and East Tennessee has a very good reputation for teacher training."

Looking at the transcripts, I brought along, the dean says, "Mr. Berger, I see you were asked to leave Baruch College. What can you tell me about that?"

"I was immature when I first went to college. I didn't study like I should have and that's how come I got the grades I did. I guess, to make my folks happy, I majored in business, except it didn't work. In the end, it made us all sad. I learned that I should go for what interests me. I know what that is now, education. Coming here is a new start for me. I intend to do well."

Smiling slightly, he tells me, "If we take you, we take all of you, the good grades and the bad ones."

Just before we finish, he leans in, and says, "Mark, we have a quiet, peaceful university here. You'll do well to remember that and know that we do not want nor do we need outside agitators causing us problems. Understand?"

"Yes, sir. I want to become a teacher, a really good one, that's why I want to go to school here."

"Well, you're right, we do have an excellent education department."

He says they'll notify me in a few weeks, but the way he looks me right in the eye and shakes my hand, I know I'm in.

Before heading to the airport, I drive around Johnson City. I see lots of small houses, small yards, and big churches. Finding a park, I get out to think, but I'm distracted by a teenager playing with his shaggy, oversized brown dog. The boy throws a ball and the dog takes off after it, wagging its tail. I notice there's something odd about the way it runs. Retrieving the ball, Big Brown races back. As it gets closer, I see it only has three legs—two up front, one in the back. Poor dog is my first thought, but that's not right. This dog just may be the happiest one I've ever seen.

Flying home, I think, things in Brooklyn are definitely not cool. I'm kind of a mess, too. If I come here, I can have a new life. I can be like that dog, wagging its tail while it chases the ball.

November 1966

DEENA

I'm in Junior's, a popular, downtown Brooklyn eatery, using one of the pay phones upstairs to arrange a shipment of two kilos of Hawaiian pot from Spider who's in California. Instead of dropping dimes into the coin slot, I'm using slugs, specifically #1 flat brass washers.

After working out the details, I head downstairs for something to eat. On the way up is this beauty with long, ash blond hair, dressed in a tan pin-striped suit, open-necked blue blouse, loosened tie, and heels. If models were 5'2", she'd be fronting for Dior.

I hand her some slugs and say, "Use these." To my surprise, she takes them.

Sitting down at the counter, I keep an eye on the wall mirror. Sure enough, a couple of minutes later, she marches directly over to me. Looking spooked, she glances around and whispers, "They work. You could get arrested for using slugs."

Whispering back, I say, "You mean *we* could get arrested. If you don't turn me in, I won't turn you in. Listen, if you let me buy you dessert, I promise I won't tell you how adorable you look when you're scared."

She slides onto a stool. "I'm Deena." We order Junior's famous cheesecake, delicious. Getting up to leave, she gives me her phone number. "If you ask me out, I'll say yes."

So I do. And she does. Going to her favorite Italian restaurant, she suggests lobster *fra diavolo*, fabulous. We click—our families are a drag, our friends are nuts. We're both ready for a change and, well, we're digging each other. Over the next few weeks, we talk a lot, but I avoid mentioning that I've applied to East Tennessee State University.

December brings a blizzard of changes. Deena moves out of her mother's house and takes an apartment near Prospect Park. I lose my place after a couple I let stay there forgets to turn off the bathtub faucet, flooding the cellar. John, the super, tells me, "Landlord says you got a week to clear out."

Deena invites me to move in with her. We're feeling good enough about how things are going between us that we decide to share the news with our folks.

Her mother screams, "Deena, you're ruining your life and your reputation."

My parents tell us we should have our heads examined. Which kind of seals the deal.

On a snowy December night, we move me into her cozy, quiet apartment.

Then the acceptance letter from E.T.S.U. arrives. I only have ten days to respond. The admissions packet states, "Only seniors and married undergraduate students may live off campus." I'm not fazed at first, because I generally think rules are more like recommendations—whether I follow them is up to me. Then I remember Dean Beardsley emphatically saying the university doesn't want outsiders like me causing any problems. Still, could I live in a dorm? Impossible.

Here are my options: Stay in Brooklyn, go to Tennessee alone or invite Deena along. Brooklyn? The scene's gotten too dangerous, my mind's made up, it's time to split. Tennessee solo? Talk about being a stranger in a strange land. Deena along? Things might be easier and more fun. Do I want to ask her? Would she even want to go?

Taking her to my favorite Chinese restaurant for *Wah-Shoo-Op*, braised duck, I start, "I've something important to tell you."

Her jaw drops, "Are you breaking up with me?"

"No, no. Couple of months ago, I applied to East Tennessee State University. Long story short, I can get out of college a year early if I go there. Well, I just got the acceptance letter and now I have to decide."

"East Tennessee? Where's that? You're doing what?"

"I'm not sure I'm doing anything, but I've got a decision to make."

"Two decisions to make."

"OK. But, babe, if I go, I'll be back by summer."

"If you go, you're gone." She starts bawling, tears falling like autumn leaves. "I've never been this happy before. You too, I know it. How could you?"

I feel super guilty, and considering some of the things I've done, that says a lot.

Lips quivering, she says, "Please, let me come along. My job's just a job. Nothing's holding me here. I want to be with you."

Then she drops the L word. "Mark, I love you."

I falter, then I fold. "We'll have to tell them we're married."

Deena's starts kissing me and doesn't stop until the waiter brings our two fortune cookies. Hers says, "Perseverance furthers," and we laugh.

The second one I throw away and comment, "Sometimes, you have to write your own fortune."

December 1966

PUFF

In February, Deena and I buy a '53 Chevy, hitch a U-Haul trailer to it, pack it full with our belongings, and drive southwest for 640 miles to Johnson City, the home of East Tennessee State University.

With surprising ease, we rent a small house not far from campus. As we unpack, we're startled by a noise at our back door. Opening it, we find this black-and-white mutt sitting at attention while its tail furiously slaps the ground.

Deena says, "What do we have here?" and starts to pet it. She likes dogs, her family had owned several, but I'm standoffish. The only pet I ever had was a ceramic cocker spaniel *tchotchke* my mother kept on an end table and I named "Pal."

The mutt rolls onto its back. "We've got a boy here," Deena says.

"What're we going to do with him?"

"First, we gotta get him some dog food. Then he's gonna need a name."

"Whoa—he must belong to someone."

"I've a feeling he does—us." Laughing, she gives me a little kiss.

Going to a Kroger's supermarket, we stock up on stuff for the house and dog food for the pooch. Deena sets out the dog chow and water in the kitchen and calls him.

The dog comes to the door, but that's as far as he'll go. Moving his food under an eave out back, we watch him eat as Deena leans softly against me. She says, "Maybe the last tenants just drove off and abandoned him."

"Gone in a puff of smoke. I've got it, let's call him Puff. Maybe he's a magic dragon in disguise."

Monday, I head off to my first day of classes. My dad's advice was simple: "Keep your eyes and ears open and your mouth shut." My first professor's Southern twang is so heavy that I can barely make sense of anything he says. I resolve to come to class prepared so that I have a shot at following the lectures.

The campus is pretty and mellow. No one seems in a hurry. The students hold doors, smile and nod hello to one another, including to a newcomer like me.

Over lunch, Deena details her plans to make our place cozy. "It's our first house together, let's make it nice," she says.

Since her ideas involve work and money, I say, "We're not even sure if we're staying past this trimester."

"Come on, Mark, let's stay positive here."

So, we negotiate a compromise—we'll contribute $50 apiece to fixing up the place and when that money is gone, we'll have another conversation about doing stuff.

Getting into the car for the trip to a nearby department store, I open the back door for Puff, but he won't get in. I put a dog biscuit on the backseat. Still no go. As we drive down our street, he runs alongside the car until we reach the corner. Then he turns back home.

Returning with our housewares, we're startled to find our frontyard bestrewn with towels, tops, and jeans. Sitting in the middle of this mess is Puff, proud as a lion bringing home his first zebra.

Grinning, Deena says, "Oh, Puff, how sweet, but see, we have our own stuff."

Surveying the adjacent backyards, I notice one clothesline with only socks and underwear on it and a bunch of clothes pins scattered on the ground.

"That must be the place," I say.

Gathering the laundry, we knock on that neighbor's door, not knowing what to expect. A rail-thin woman in her twenties answers. Pointing toward Puff, we explain what happened. Instead of getting angry, she laughs, "Back home, the goats get everything."

Several days later, a plumber comes over to fix the hot water heater. When he finishes, we thank him, and he says, "Where y'all from?" We tell him Brooklyn.

"Well, my wife, Debbie, and me would be right honored if you and the missus would come over for dinner. We don't get much chance to talk to people from New York City."

We sidestep the invitation, citing school work and other obligations. After he leaves, I say, "So this is what they call Southern hospitality. We've only been here a couple of days and we have a cute house, a dog and school's starting . . ."

"Yeah, and we have things to make our home homey, we've met a neighbor, gotten a dinner invitation, and I just got called 'the missus.' Pretty cool."

"Totally cool," I say. "One thing's for sure, babe, we're not in Brooklyn anymore."

Spring 1967

COMRADES

"This is going to be interesting," I say to Deena, pointing to an article in *The Collegian*. "It says here, 'Allen Ginsberg, the poet, will be doing a reading on campus.'"

"He's kind of a legend, right? So what's the problem?"

"Yeah, he's celebrated and despised. His poetry's great, but it's what he writes about that's got the establishment against him. He's totally honest about his own life—drugs, pinko politics, and his sex life. He doesn't apologize for any of it. Last time I saw him was at Judson Memorial Church, at a poetry reading. His lover, Peter Orlovski, stripped down to his bikini underwear and started screaming that Ginsberg was a bastard because he was giving blowjobs to everyone but him. . . . Oh, by the way, the time before that time, I was in their apartment."

That got Deena's attention. "What were you doing there? I'm afraid to ask."

"Nah, nothing like that. Spider's friends with this writer, Peter Stafford, who knows Ginsberg. One time we're hanging out at Stafford's place and he has to tell Ginsberg something, so he invited us along. Ginsberg's cool—instead of talking about himself, he wanted to know what we were doing with our lives."

"When's the reading?"

"Supposed to be next week, but who knows what'll happen once the administration finds out who's been invited."

Sure enough, the *Johnson City Press-Chronicle* picks up the story from the campus newspaper, running a picture of Ginsberg, looking like the beatnik poet he is, along with an article focusing on the things I told Deena about. Local ministers chastise the university's administration for inviting the poet to the college.

Next day, the dean issues a statement asserting East Tennessee State University's support of academic freedom, but concluding that Ginsberg's "lifestyle" is out of step with Johnson City's community values. The English department hustles and finds an off-campus site for the reading. And so, the world's most famous Jewish, beatnik, homosexual, vegetarian, pot-smoking, poet gets booked into the banquet room of the Long Horn Steak House.

In the six weeks we've been here, we've become friends with some artists, craftsmen, and musicians. On the day of the reading, Deena cooks up a big pot of chili to feed a bunch of our new pals, after which we all head on over to the Long Horn.

Passing a couple of uniformed cops in the parking lot, we go to the banquet room, which is as charming as a shoebox. Ginsberg is seated at a table holding a large notebook. The room's almost filled, impressive for a poetry reading.

Lance, the leader of a local folk band, says to me, "I'll bet there are undercover cops here."

"Probably. Just like in New York."

After an English professor's tepid introduction, Ginsberg steps to the lectern. He begins with "Howl," whose opening lines are his most well-known: "I saw the best minds of my generation destroyed by madness, starving hysterical naked." Then on to his poem "America" where the poet wonders: when will he be able to go into a store and buy what he needs with his good looks?

An hour passes; the audience is riveted. Introducing his last poem, Ginsberg says, "I wrote 'Wichita Vortex Sutra' in Wichita, Kansas, a year ago. Had I waited I might have composed it with Johnson City in mind: 'Kansas! Kansas! Shuddering at last / PERSON appearing in Kansas!'"

When he finishes, there are several hearty rounds of applause. He bows and says, "*Shaanti*." Peace.

Deena and I linger toward the back of the line of people waiting to meet Ginsberg. Getting up to him, I say, "Thanks. Great reading. I was wondering, do you remember me? Last year, Peter Stafford brought me and a couple of my friends over to your apartment on East 7th Street."

Peering at me, he says, "Yes, yes. The Timothy Leary thing. What're you doing here?"

"Brooklyn got to be too much, had to get away, so I transferred to East Tennessee State."

With a furrowed brow, Ginsberg takes our hands in his and looking intently at us, he says, "Just be careful." Then, smiling, he continues, "It's so wonderful to see my comrades everywhere I go."

Outside, our group is waiting. Lance says, "Wow, you know him."

"Well, he's a friend of a friend of a friend."

Deena says, "Mark's full of surprises."

Spring 1967

THE LITTLES

Lonnie Little, who plays banjo in our friend Lance's band, is a passenger in our clanky, chattering, blue-and-white '53 Chevy as we drive over to Daylight Donuts to get some coffee.

"This car sounds real bad," Lonnie says. When we park, he pops open the hood. Looking at the engine, he shakes his head. "Tell you what. How 'bout coming home with me this weekend? My buddy Charlie's a real good car mechanic. He can fix your car while my folks can meet some of my new college friends."

We're in. Friday evening finds us rolling across the North Carolina state line and into the spectacular Blue Ridge Mountains. Passing through Boone, we head north to West Jefferson, Lonnie's home.

The DJ on the bluegrass station we're tuned to says, "Coming up—the rush hour traffic report."

"Wait'll y'all hear this," Lonnie says,

I'm wondering what traffic there is to report—six cars headed north, three headed south?

After a banjo fanfare, the announcer intones, "As always, the traffic report is brought to you by Big D, Donnie Little, owner of Little's Well Service: Where big water problems are fixed for only a little."

Lonnie grins proudly. "Big D's my dad."

~

Mrs. Little, all blond and smiley, greets us at the door. She's busy cooking dinner. At first, when Deena offers to help, Mrs. Little seems somewhat reluctant, but when Deena says, "Back home, I'm the salad maker," Mrs. Little hands her an apron.

Big D, built like a gas pump, comes in and pumps my hand. "I hear that little Chevy's got a problem or two. Well, Charlie Watson'll fix 'er up right fine."

When Mrs. Little finishes up her cooking, her teenage daughter, Linda, who looks more like her mom's younger sister, goes back and forth bringing the fried chicken, yams, cornbread, and fresh salad, topped with Deena's homemade dressing, to the table. Yum. Afterwards I start to rise to help the women clear the table, but Lonnie's glance tells me to sit back down, and I do.

Next morning, Mrs. Little mentions she's sewing Linda a dress. Deena asks, "Can I watch? I just bought a secondhand sewing machine to make my own clothes, but I'm not sure how to use it."

"Honey, I guess there's a few things I could show you."

So while Deena goes for her sewing lesson, Lonnie and I drop the car off at Watson's Garage, then we drive around picking up hardware and other things Big D needs for his business. Everywhere we go, everyone knows my friend.

Around lunchtime, we check in with Charlie. "Lonnie, if you can grind out these valves, I reckon, I'll get it done today."

Going to his dad's shop, Lonnie gets to work. By midafternoon, the valves are back in the mechanic's hands. Before dinner, we go to pick up the car.

"What do I owe you?" I ask.

"The Watsons and the Littles go back a long way. So just pay for the parts and we'll call it even."

"Even? Look, no disrespect, but where I come from, Brooklyn, New York, the way we show appreciation is by paying people hard cash, so here's some appreciation." Handing him a $100, he stuffs the money into his pocket without counting and thanks me.

After dinner, Linda's new boyfriend, Roger, arrives. We all go into the living room, where Linda sits down at an upright piano, her mom takes out a beautifully carved dulcimer, and Big D tunes a Martin guitar. Lonnie unpacks his banjo. Roger goes out to his pickup and brings in a fiddle. Lonnie hands Deena and me tambourines.

Launching into the Carter Family classic "Hello Stranger," Mrs. Little sings in a high nasal voice, "Hello, stranger, put your loving hand in mine." Folk songs follow spirituals, until finally, Big D leads us all in "Will the Circle Be Unbroken."

While everyone's packing up, Linda catches her mom's eye, "Don't Roger play nice?" A question with clearly larger implications.

I tell Lonnie, "Feels like we just sat in at the Grand Ole Opry."

"This here's a regular Saturday night at home."

At breakfast on Sunday, we thank the family for their hospitality.

"Come back anytime," says Mrs. Little.

Trying to make some conversation, I point to the mountain that dominates the view from the picture window. "What's its name?"

"Used to be called Nigger Mountain," Big D replies, "but then they said that won't do, so now it's Nigra Mountain, but that don't satisfy 'em neither, so it looks like it'll be called Mount Jefferson."

Looking at Deena, I raise my eyebrows ever so slightly while the rest of the family just goes on eating.

Back on the road, I say, "The South's going to take some getting used to."

Deena nods in agreement.

"Right pretty, ain't it?" says Lonnie.

"That too."

May 1967

Driving through the Blue Ridge Mountains in early spring, I'm overwhelmed by its physical beauty. Mountainsides are filled with trees, meadows bloom with flowers, and streams circulate through the landscape like the arteries in our body. In a moment of reverie, I imagine Deena and me living out here, far from towns and people, working hard, living simply.

I'm riding with Lonnie, Rob, and Bill of the Ridge Riders. Deena and our friend Keri are up ahead with Lance in his station wagon—a '54 Ford Woody, which once carried his surfing gear to Virginia Beach and now serves as the band transport. We're headed to Lees-McCrae Junior College for a gig.

The road corkscrews up a mountain and when it reaches the summit, there's a sign pointing to the college entrance. The campus, green and sizable, is filled with students enjoying the spring weather—playing catch, reading, hanging out. Pulling up to the gym, a heavyset, student in a button-down blue shirt and tan chinos is waiting for us.

"Hi, I'm George McDougal. Pleased y'all were able to make it."

"What an absolutely beautiful location," Deena says.

"You might not know this, but Lees-McCrae College has the highest elevation of any campus east of the Mississippi."

Carrying the musical equipment inside, Bill whispers, "But I bet we're higher than anyone else on campus."

After setting up the mics and playing through a couple of songs, we take a short hike and find a quiet spot to relax. Rob passes around a joint. Returning to the campus, we meander into the student union. I hear the sounds of billiard balls striking each other and, sure enough, they have a two-table pool room. On one, four guys are playing. The other one's empty.

Lance suggests nine ball. Deena and I are game, but our friends head back outside. She and I have played pool a number of times and she's good. She chooses a pool cue and rolls it on the table to make sure the cue's not warped. The players at the other table glance sideways. Lance breaks and makes the one ball. I knock down the two and three. Deena makes the four on a bank shot and then runs the rest of the table. The Lees-McCrae guys have stopped playing.

I rack the balls. Deena breaks, sinking the three. Then she makes the one, two, and four, before missing. We play once more and she wins. I can't believe how well she's playing.

"Excuse me, Miss," one of the boys says, "but where'd you learn to shoot like that?"

"Spinella's Pool Room in Brooklyn."

"Do girls shoot pool in poolrooms in Brooklyn?"

"Only if they're good enough."

When we leave, I say, "You played like you were on fire."

"I know. I amazed myself. I wanted to show them that girls can do a lot of things boys don't think they can."

"The game doesn't take strength," says Lance. "What it takes is a sharp eye, a steady stroke, and poise, and boy, you poised those good ol' boys good."

Lonnie tells us we've been invited to the frat house for a buffet dinner. When we get there, George points the way to the dining room, "Whyn't y'all help yourselves."

"Much appreciated," says Lonnie.

The buffet has southern fare, like fried chicken, biscuits, and corn, but also lasagna. As I get a plate, I spy Deena at the last table, excitedly waving me over.

Pointing at a pink platter, she says, "Look at this—lox."

My jaw drops. "Oh, my God, that's got to be a couple of pounds of the stuff. The most my mom would ever buy was a quarter pound and that was for the four of us."

George comes over, "Caterer told me it's real popular, somewhere."

"Back in Brooklyn," I say.

"Tell you what, y'all can take it all."

And so, in a heartbeat, Deena and I become richer in smoked salmon than we ever dreamed possible.

The band kicks off with Muddy Waters' "I'm a Man." Lance sings lead while Rob does a so-so imitation of James Cotton's harmonica playing. Next, Lonnie plays "Foggy Mountain Breakdown" on his banjo and most everyone claps along.

I note the frat brothers' long sideburns descending from their short haircuts and imagine they're doing their part to come across as being a little hipper. I wonder if it's tough for these guys to look more like their peers in New York and San Francisco, because, maybe for southerners, identifying with the larger culture may feel too much like surrendering.

Bill's drum roll introduces Chuck Berry's "Oh Carol." Four miniskirted girls take to the dance floor, just having fun. The band is trying to find its groove, but jumping from blues to folk to rock confuses the crowd.

Finally, Lance announces the next number will be the last and waves Keri onstage. Deena and I look at each other in surprise. Our friend launches into a spirited version of "I'm a Woman," a Leiber and Stoller song that Maria Muldaur sings on a Jim Kweskin and the Jug Band album. Keri grins as she belts out the line that promises the guys in the audience that if she can make a dress out of a feedbag, she can "make a man out of you."

The guys stand to check out the singer, while their girls smile knowingly at each other—this song could well be their anthem. Keri gets the biggest ovation of the night.

"Good job," George says as he hands Lance the band's pay.

Keri pulls Deena to the side, "How was I?"

"Keri, you were great, you stole the show."

"I was so nervous, it feels like all I did the past few days was practice that song."

"It showed."

As we load the Woody, I say, "I like how you kicked off with 'I'm a Man' and finished with 'I'm a Woman'—cool."

Deena gets into Lonnie's car with me for the ride back to Johnson City. She asks, "How'd you think it went?"

"They probably won't remember the Ridge Riders, they might remember Keri singing that song, but I am sure that not one of those boys in the poolroom will ever forget the Brooklyn chick who shot pool like a pro."

Spring 1967

SHORE TIME

When the trimester ends at ETSU, Deena and I return to Brooklyn She gets a job in the office of a toy company. Through my mom, I get one as a water meter reader. We're saving up as much money as possible to take back to Tennessee in September.

So when Harry Roberts, one of our Tennessee friends, invites us to spend a weekend with him and his family at their home on the Jersey Shore, we jump at the chance. That's how, on this sweltering July night, Deena and I find ourselves stuck in traffic on the Garden State Parkway, en route to Wildwood.

Waiting for the tie-up to ease up, Deena says, "I remember one time when I was a kid, my parents took me to the Jersey Shore. Left when I was five, got there when I was six."

"Look, traffic's moving. You sure worked a lot of overtime this week."

"My boss, Edith, never wants to go home—problems with her husband. Mark, you appreciate me, right?"

"When we get to Harry's, I'm aiming to show you how much."

"I used to think working in offices was so cool, but not anymore. Now I want to become a craftsman, like Izzy and Norma. Earn money by making pretty things."

When we pull up, Harry is sitting on the porch sipping a beer. With his reddish blond hair, thin moustache, athletic body and great smile, he's handsome enough to be an actor. Next trimester, we're planning on helping each other out by taking a meteorology course together. After catching up, he shows us to our room. Deena and I climb into bed. Tired from work and the drive, I fall asleep before my head hits the pillow.

At breakfast, Harry's mom serves us bacon and eggs and then continues doing household chores. His older brother, Tommy, comes in. He's just become the "& Son" in their dad's plumbing business and the two men lay out the day's calls. We're basically ignored—northern hospitality, I guess.

With the sun climbing the ladder toward noon, Harry says, "Let's go swimming." The beach is busy, but not crowded. Kids congregate in small groups on beach blankets.

Looking around, I say, "In Brooklyn, the beaches are packed tight—it's kind of like the apartment houses are laid out flat on the sand. It's a trip. Each blanket is filled with different kinds of people and they're all listening to different radio stations."

Deena adds, "Yeah, rock, Latin, R&B, opera."

"Here it's more like the private houses—y'know, fewer people and there's space between the blankets."

"And everyone's tuned to the same station," Harry says.

After dinner, we go to the famous Wildwood boardwalk. It's like a sandy Times Square—loud, crowded, and a tourist hustle every step of the way. Harry bumps into some people he went to high school with. They invite us to join them at the Hurricane, a nearby bar. We tell Harry to go ahead, we want to walk on the beach and will join them later.

We're happy to be alone. We wander down to the shoreline and stroll along the water's edge with our arms around each other. With the moon smiling down, I turn Deena toward me and we kiss. Lying down on the warm sand, we make out like a couple of teenagers. After a while, we sit side by side on the sand.

"I'm so happy we're together," she says.

Embracing again, I say, "Deena, things make sense with you."

At Sunday's breakfast, Harry's grandparents show up and start complaining about some of the tourists. "They park their cars anywhere. Who knows what they're thinking? They think traffic signs, speed limits, turn signals don't apply to them."

"And their kids, no manners whatsoever," Granny says. "Yesterday, coming out of the grocery store, two of their brats almost bowled me over."

Harry's parents nod in agreement.

Bewildered, I say, "I'm sorry, but this is my first time here. Who're you talking about?"

"Those miserable French-Canadians, that's who," Gramps replies,

Suppressing a laugh, Deena and I excuse ourselves from the table. Later, I tell Harry, "Lonnie's parents had the same kind of attitude toward blacks."

"That's why I'm cool with Tennessee," Harry says. "Northerners, southerners, Catholics, Protestants, Hindus, Moslems, it doesn't matter. Seems like most people need to look down their noses at other people, but that's not what I'm about."

Before we leave, he says, "I've been thinking. In September, I'm going to be a senior, so I can live off campus. Maybe if you find a big enough house, I could rent a room."

Deena's look says she fine with the idea, so I say, "Sure."

"Cool," Harry replies.

"Let's go sit in traffic," Deena says as we climb into our trusty '53 Chevy.

July 1967

"I miss Johnson City," Deena says to me. We're sitting on the sand, enjoying the tide splash onto Coney Island's moonlit beach.

"Me, too. Funny, us liking a place like that."

"Well, we've made cool friends, school's going good, and it's beautiful."

"Only thing is, I just don't like us lying to everyone about being married."

"We could do something about that," she says, with a shy smile.

"What? Tell the truth and get booted out of college?"

"No, it could be the truth." She's laughing now.

Catching her drift, I start laughing, too, until we're both hysterical. But is it really such a crazy idea? We love each other and we're great together.

"Let's do it," I say, gathering my composure.

"Mark, are you asking me to marry you?"

"I believe I am."

"Then, yes, yes, yes." Now she's beaming. We kiss and hug and kiss some more.

My future mother-in-law is friends with a judge and he agrees to marry us in his chambers in the Supreme Court building in downtown Brooklyn. So, two weeks later, we're husband and wife. I'm 23, Deena's 21.

~

Returning to Johnson City at the beginning of September, with money saved from our summer jobs and wedding presents, we're radiating happiness. Both of us are eagerly looking forward to a full year at East Tennessee State University. I'm hoping to graduate at the end of the summer session and Deena is planning on taking an art and design class. The way we're feeling, if I could get a teaching job around here, we might stay on for a while.

Life feels so exciting that getting high becomes less important to us. So we only bring back a couple of joints and some uppers, which I've used in the past when I needed to put in an all-nighter. Also, we've brought our two cats along—Snowflake and Blackjack. Deena's mom took care of them while we were here in the spring.

Repeating the good luck we had before, we quickly find a house to rent on Spruce Street—situated in a working-class neighborhood—two bedrooms with a little study in the back for me. We retrieve the furniture we stored in Izzy and Norma's garage. To reduce expenses, we ask Harry Roberts if he is still interested in moving in with us. He is.

Over pizza, Deena and Harry discover they share a birthday, September 23. Harry says, "Talk about being in sync. Let's have a combined birthday party."

"Sounds perfect," responds Deena.

"We better get to work, if the house is gonna be ready in time," I suggest.

In the next couple of weeks, we go to the Salvation Army and to garage sales and buy some furniture and knickknacks, including an old desk and a stuffed, gray plaid chair for my study. Deciding we can furnish the living room ourselves, Harry and I build a couple of plywood couches with canopies which Deena decorates with colorful fabric and pillows. We string colored, flashing lights around the room and put up a psychedelic poster to create an ethereal effect.

On party night, our friends fill up our home, some bringing friends of their own. If houses could smile, this one would be grinning ear to ear. Our pals, the Ridge Riders, play a couple of songs, then someone puts *Sergeant Pepper* on the stereo. Cadillac Jack, Harry's buddy, hands me a beer, pats me on the back, and shouts in my ear, "Great party." In the kitchen, there's Deena and Norma giggling together. My wife throws me a kiss.

Making my way back to the living room, I notice this stranger in a denim cowboy shirt sitting by himself in a corner.

Assuming he's a friend of a friend I approach him to introduce myself. Just then the front door bursts open and cops storm in screaming: "This is a raid. Everyone down." Some cops have their revolvers out, others carry billy clubs.

Last in is the captain who looks like a two-legged lizard. The guy in the denim shirt nods toward me and like a punch in the gut, I realize he's an undercover cop. The lizard hands me the search warrant. Some officers frisk the party goers. Others ransack the house.

In the confusion, I slide into our bedroom to grab the uppers and go to flush them down the toilet, but two cops stop me and strip the vial from my grip.

They take me and the drugs to the captain.

"What're these?" he demands,

I just glare at him. He looks like he'd love to deck me, but having a houseful of witnesses must make him think twice.

A minute later, Deena, Norma, Gwen, and the other women, all in handcuffs, are led past. They are freaked out. I tell Deena, "Don't talk to anyone, except a lawyer."

Harry, Lance, Lonnie, Izzy, Cadillac Jack, me, and the rest of the men are handcuffed and jostled outside. The flashing lights of the squad cars and paddy wagons illuminate the street. Gawking neighbors fill the sidewalks.

I mutter to myself, "This is one big fucking deal."

Most of us men are taken to a dank and dirty holding cell, maybe 20' by 15', at police headquarters.

Lonnie says, "Since when is it illegal to have a birthday party?"

No one responds. What is there to say?

Sitting in groups of twos and threes, they talk quietly among themselves, stealing looks in my direction. I keep to myself.

Early Sunday morning, the *Johnson City Press-Chronicle* is passed through the bars. We're the banner headline: "23 People Arrested . . . Raid Nets Marijuana." The reporter seems to make it his business to detail things that would most horrify the paper's readership: "psychedelic colors," "flashing lights," "barbiturates drugs," "guitars," and books titles like William James's *Varieties of Religious Experience* and Lenny Bruce's *How to Talk Dirty and Influence People.*

As the day goes on, one by one, my cellmates get released. Finally, it's Deena's and my turn. After making arrangements for bail, we're free—for now.

Deena says, "I can't go back to the house."

Before I can respond, I notice a couple sitting on a bench near the entrance to the station. They look out of place. I'm startled to realize that it's Dr. Davis, my history professor from last term, and his wife. We'd met them at the Allen Ginsberg poetry reading. Coming over to us, they say they've been waiting for us to be released. Unbelievably, they invite us to stay with them. Gratefully, we accept.

At their house, Dr. Davis says, "Please call me Richard."

"I'm Sandy," says his wife, extending her hand. "Would you care for something to eat?"

"Not right now," I say. "We need some time alone."

Showing us into their guest room, Sandy says, "Y'all help yourselves to anything you want. If you need us, we'll be in our bedroom."

We thank them profusely.

Deena falls on the bed wailing. "What's going to happen to us? Are we going to prison?"

Collapsing next to her, I'm devastated. We embrace each other with tears streaming down our faces—afraid of what our future holds and mourning the sudden death of our new, wonderful life.

September 1967

Startled awake by a nightmare, I look around and realize I'm not being chased by wild dogs. Instead I'm in bed and Deena's asleep beside me. I register that we're in Richard and Sandy Davis's guest bedroom after getting bailed out on Sunday evening, following Saturday night's bust at our house. So today must be Monday.

Wandering into the kitchen, I find a note on the table. "Mark and Deena, Please make yourselves at home. But, don't go outside. Don't answer the door. Don't answer the phone. See you at noon. R&S."

They've left coffee, I pour myself a cup and then take a shower. Deena is awake, looking totally shaken. I go to hug her, she pulls away, but I gently pull her back. "Babe, listen, it's just you and me. We've got to be solid for each other."

Embracing me for all she's worth, her tears tumble down. "I cried the whole time I was in that disgusting cell. I had to share it with some drunken lady. What about you?"

"Quiet, like a funeral. Almost all the guys were in with me. Some looked at me like I was contaminated. I just kept to myself. Look, we can't admit to anyone that we had stuff."

"I know," she says. "What're we going to do now?"

"We're going to eat breakfast."

At 12, on the dot, the Davises return.

Deena says, "You saved us. We can't thank you enough."

Sandy replies, "We just had to help."

"The college plans on suspending everyone arrested," Richard says.

"We're lepers," I say.

"Worse, hippies. I think the administration believes one puff of marijuana and the whole student body will become addicted."

Sandy shows us today's paper—we're still the lead story. They've included two photographs: the first of two detectives "looking at the evidence seized," the other of our living room, including our white cat Snowflake. The last sentence of that caption reads, "The cat on the bed has the initials 'J.C.' painted on its forehead."

"What're they crazy?" Deena says. "Snowflake has black markings, we would never paint her. What's J.C.? Johnson City?"

"Jesus Christ," I say. "They're making us out to be some weird religious cult."

Richard reads the article aloud. The lizard, Captain Tipton, is quoted: "two ounces of marijuana . . . large quantity of marijuana cigarettes . . . various barbiturates . . . amphetamines . . . Berger is formerly of New York."

The District Attorney weighs in, "We're after the vultures who're hooking our kids on drugs." The preliminary hearing is scheduled for Thursday.

"Tipton's lying through his teeth. He's a dirty liar," I yell. "What two ounces of pot?"

"Can they do that? Can they just lie about everything?" Deena asks.

"You need a lawyer," Richard says.

"An American Civil Liberties Union lawyer," Sandy adds.

We call the Nashville ACLU chapter and get referrals to two local attorneys. Calling the first, he tells me, "Sorry, I'm in the middle of a big case. Is Lester Clayter on your list?"

"Yes, he is."

"Call him."

Clayter's secretary puts us through right away.

"Y'all better come here today, after hours, let's say six o'clock," Clayter says with a deep drawl. "Ring the bell twice. And bring that damn cat with the paint job. This I have to see for myself."

After Richard and Sandy leave, I tell Deena, "We need some of our things. I can go to the house myself."

"No way. I'm coming too."

We have a cab drop us off a block away. Funny, it looks like a regular, ordinary street, not the deadend alley it has become for us.

Inside our house, it looks like a whirlwind passed through—furniture is overturned, drawers emptied on the floor, pillows cut open, everything's in a heap.

"This was our home, and they just tore it all apart. The bastards." Deena says.

We start stuffing clothes and important papers into suitcases and bags. Then I see our stereo is gone. So is the stained-glass window we bought at a yard sale. Deena rushes in, "They stole my jewelry box with the gold necklace my Nana gave me."

The back door's wide open.

"We'd better get out of here before they come back."

"Wait. Where are our cats?" Hurriedly, we look everywhere, but they're gone.

Getting into our car, which is still parked out front, we drive around the neighborhood looking for them, no luck. Deena's head is between her knees, she hysterical again. I pull over and try to comfort her, but she pulls away. I park in the rear of a bread factory, away from other cars, and give her some time. I feel miserable too, but I'm not letting myself give in to it. My mind is racing trying to figure out ways we can get out of this thing.

"I promise we'll come back every day until we find them," I say. But as I make this promise, I realize that I've just lied to Deena, for the very first time.

"What do we do? Call the cops?"

"We'll ask the lawyer."

We drive to Clayter's office. I ring the bell twice and this big guy comes to the door.

"Mr. Clayter?" I ask.

"Call me Lester."

"That's my middle name."

September 1967

Lester Clayter, wearing well-worn, brown cowboy boots, is in his thirties and jumbo-sized. On his desk sits a varsity football helmet. "Used to play guard, but my knees had other ideas. Now I stick with golf. Cat in the car?"

"Missing," I say. "Last night we stayed with friends. This afternoon was our first time back at the house and it's like a tornado hit it—it's a total mess, some of our stuff was stolen, and the back door was left wide open. The cats must've split."

"We were ripped off," Deena says emphatically. "They took the necklace my Nana gave me, our stereo." She tears up. "Lots more. Should we call the police?"

Lester shakes his head, "Not much point. All that'll happen is the newspaper will write another story about all your *unusual* possessions."

"Lester, they're dirty liars, no one painted 'J.C' on Snowflake. She just had black markings on her forehead," Deena says.

"Well the cat's not on trial. But one day you might be. To most people here in the Bible Belt, those initials mean the world to them. If folks believe you did that to your cat, they'll believe the other nefarious deeds you are being accused of."

"There goes getting a fair trial," I say.

Lester steers the conversation elsewhere. "I have two rules for my clients: Rule number one: Pay me what you owe me without delay. I can't defend you, if I'm chasing you for money. Rule number two: Tell me everything. The more you hide, the worse it gets."

He's experienced, sharp, and sympathetic. In our straits, a Legal Aid attorney is out of the question, so I write him a check for his retainer.

"Now tell me the story in all its gory details."

I start. "I tried to dump some uppers . . . um, amphetamines . . . down the toilet and got caught. But we had almost no pot. No way Tipton's telling the truth that we had two ounces of marijuana, plus all kinds of joints . . . um, cigarettes."

"Tipton," he grumbles. "I don't know how that snake grew legs, but I do know he gets so worked up about throwing people in jail, he sometimes forgets there's something called the truth and something else called the United States Constitution."

"Which reminds me," I say. "Was the search warrant legal?"

"That's the first thing I'll take a look at."

"What are we going to do?" Deena asks.

"Right now, they're moving like that rabbit, speeding right along, hoping to push you through the prison gates as fast as they can. My plan is to be like that turtle. We need to slow things down some, catch our breath, sort things out. Our first move is to get Thursday's preliminary hearing postponed."

"Good. Look, should I withdraw from school so we can head home?"

"Reckon, the sooner your tail's in the breeze, the better. The college, the police, and the DA will be mighty glad to be rid of y'all. They'll sleep better knowing you're not planning on becoming Tennesseans, but first I'll need to get the court's permission. Now think very carefully, have you ever sold any drugs to anyone here?"

"Never," we say.

"Last thing, I hope you two are legally married, and can prove it, because here, in the Volunteer State, volunteering to live together, co-habiting, is against the law."

Deena and I look at each other and smile. Since getting arrested, smiles have become a luxury.

"Who wudda thunk?" I say.

Deena says, "I can bring you our marriage license tomorrow."

"I'd be much obliged."

Tuesday's *Johnson City Press-Chronicle* recounts the details of the arrest and includes Tennessee's sentencing requirements for felony drug possession—a mandatory two to five years in the state penitentiary.

That afternoon, Deena asks Clayter, "Would they do that to us?"

"Can't predict the future, but I'm on the job. Been talking to DA Bowman and to John Washington, your roommate's attorney."

In Wednesday's newspaper, we're on page 14—progress.

Clayter calls, "Preliminary hearing's been postponed until November 1. I got permission from the court for the two of you to return to New York."

We almost cheer.

We drive by the house a couple more times, but Snowflake and Blackjack are nowhere to be seen. Over the weekend, we clear out the place, giving most of our stuff away. Sunday night, we go over to Izzy and Norma's to say goodbye. Lance and Keri are there too. We all keep it light. Hard to believe that just eight days ago, we were all aglow.

Monday afternoon, on our way out of town, I go into the electric company to have our service turned off. I tell the clerk my name, she gives me the once over, then writes in the address without asking for it.

We drive in silence through the Blue Ridge Mountains as the leaves twist and fall.

October 1967

THE DANCE

On Halloween, six weeks after our arrest, we arrive in Johnson City for the preliminary hearing, at which a judge will decide if there is sufficient evidence against us for the case to go to the grand jury.

Lester said we could come and go in a day. So instead of driving, we take an airplane out of LaGuardia and switch at Washington, boarding a Piedmont Airline 24-seater. Our first stop is the mountaintop airport in Charleston, West Virginia. After a brief stop, the plane becomes airborne by speeding down the runway and, then, catapulting off the mountain. That's what I feel like doing—jumping off a mountain and disappearing into the woods.

~

Lester studies my appearance. "Mark, you need a haircut. I ain't going before Judge Cannon with you looking like that."

"I just got one."

"That there's a New York City haircut, this here's Johnson City. Go on over to Wally's Barber Shop on Market."

Deena's look says don't argue. Wally seems to agree as he spends 20 minutes giving me my second haircut in 48 hours. Looking in the mirror, I am reminded of how I looked in the fourth grade.

Back in his office, Lester brings us up to date. "I hear they're going to drop the charges against everyone, except y'all and Harry Roberts. The police and the FBI investigated campus drug use and came up with a blank."

"So why don't they just drop charges against everyone?" Deena asks.

"DA Bowman's running for re-election, so he can't be seen as abiding drugs users. And they did confiscate contraband in your home, which, by law, is presumed to be yours."

~

The courtroom's packed. Lester motions for us to come through the hinged gate into the area reserved for the prosecution and the defense. Outside the partition, sit the other 22 defendants, their family members, the press, and the curious. Harry and I shake hands.

The judge enters, we all rise. District Attorney Bowman, his hair in a buzz cut, faces the birthday party attendees.

"A reasonable doubt exists in my mind as to whether you are guilty of violating the statute regulating the use of marijuana. I believe I could have each of you indicted and possibly convicted on the charges. However, I'm going to give you the benefit of the doubt.

"The expense, embarrassment, and possible termination of your college careers have weighed heavily on my mind and have had a great deal to do with my decision.

"Should there be any reoccurrence of these parties where marijuana and other drugs are used, I will reopen these cases and let the jurors decide the question of your guilt."

A collective sigh wafts through the courtroom. They're free. Everyone's attention turns to us. Bowman puts Captain Tipton on the stand. He testifies that our house had a weird smell, that the officers "encountered people making offbeat music with bongo drums, while colored lights blinked." He states that the state lab confirmed that marijuana and other drugs were found on the premises.

Lester rises, Tipton stiffens. "Captain, can you swear that the smell you encountered was that of marijuana?"

"No, sir, I cannot."

"Did you or your officers observe anyone engaged in any illegal activity?"

"No, sir."

Turning to the judge, Lester says, "Your Honor, according to Captain Tipton here, no criminal activity was taking place at this residence, therefore I move that the court dismiss the charges against my clients."

"Motion denied."

This dance is over. The evidence presented by the prosecutor is sufficient to be presented to a grand jury.

Packing up, Clayter says under his breath, "Bowman's something. Instead of apologizing to your friends for his lack of evidence, he decided to threaten them. I guess the son of a bitch thought if someone's got to slink out of the courtroom, it might as well be them."

Mrs. Little, Lonnie's mom, is the only one who comes over to us. "Mark, Deena, I hope everything works out for y'all." I'm deeply touched by her gesture of humanity.

Outside it's raining.

"Any chance the grand jury won't indict us?" Deena asks.

"Do cows fly?" Lester responds.

"How's it look?" I ask.

"Better now that it's just three of you and you're all first timers. I got a little daylight to run through, but I still don't have that crystal ball."

We say goodbye. Lester and I shake hands. Deena gives him a hug. We smile, but it's hard.

November 1967

OPEN AND SHUT

As Lester Clayter predicted, the grand jury indicts Deena and Harry Roberts and me for felonious drug possession, which carries a minimum of two years in the state penitentiary.

Now, with our trial in two days, Deena and I sit across from our attorney, feeling like mice about to be tossed into a snake pit.

Lester goes, "After Bowman dismissed the charges against your friends, I pointed out that Tom Tipton's dream of a big drug bust was a big bust. The most they had was that a couple of East Tennessee State kids did something stupid. Bowman's got teenagers of his own. I reminded him that you were not planning on returning to Johnson City. That seemed to help. So with a dab of horse sense, we worked out a little something."

Lester leans in, looking us both in the eyes. "First, charges against Deena will be dismissed. Second, Mark pleads guilty to a misdemeanor and gets a year's probation."

Deena grabs my hand.

"What about Harry?" I ask.

"He's been offered the same deal. Now, here's where it could get a little swampy: if Harry Roberts rejects this offer and insists on going to trial, to keep your deal, you'll have to agree to testify against him. Works the other way 'round, too. If you turn this down and opt for a trial, Roberts will have to agree to testify against you."

"Turn state's evidence?"

"Mark, no jail time for us."

"Me, a rat? A fuckin' rat?"

"Son, it's a deal—to get some, you give some. Truth is, this case is open and shut. They got the evidence, the witnesses, the *Johnson City Press-Chronicle* and the holy Johnson City Police Department on their side."

Getting up, I say, "I need some air. Deena and I need to talk."
Lester nods.

My head's hanging so low it feels like it'll hit the sidewalk.
"How can I turn state's?"

"No prison time, that's how. Harry had stuff too."

"Stay here, please. I need a minute to myself to think this over."

I walk down the block, but by the time I reach the corner, I know what I have to do.

Upon entering Lester's office, I say, "I'm in. Let's just pray Harry's in too."

He waves us to our chairs. "Just got off the phone with my friend in the DA's office. Harry Roberts took the deal."

~

It starts snowing and it snows all night long.

Lester sets the stage for today's court session. "Bowman will tell Judge Hyder that the defendants have accepted a plea bargain. You and Roberts will plead guilty to the misdemeanor and apologize. Mark, make sure you apologize like you mean it. The judge may ask you a question or two. If he does, speak up and make sure to look directly at him when you respond. When that's done, he'll sentence you as agreed."

But that's not how it goes. Bowman announces that the state chemist, Dr. Taylor, is present and wants to testify.

Clayter jumps up and objects. "Your Honor, Dr. Taylor's testimony isn't relevant. The defendants have already agreed to a plea bargain."

Bowman counters, "Your Honor, Dr. Taylor drove all the way from Nashville, 300 miles, through the snow to get here. I believe we owe him the courtesy of permitting him to testify."

The judge overrules the objection.

I cease breathing. Can the judge throw out our deal and make us stand trial? I look at Lester, but he's staring at the witness.

Bowman asks, "Dr. Taylor, knowing a plea bargain had been arranged, why did you make the arduous journey to this court today?"

"Well I don't get much opportunity to participate in drug cases," Dr. Taylor replies.

He testifies, "The pills tested positive for amphetamine and about a quarter of an ounce of a leafy substance tested positive as marijuana."

"With that amount, how many marijuana cigarettes could a user make?"

Taylor stretches his neck, "Usually they cut it with tobacco, so maybe 10 or 12."

I want to shout, "What bullshit, nobody cuts pot with tobacco," but I don't.

Lester says he has no questions. The chemist steps down. The judge is silent.

To my surprise, Harry's attorney calls Harry's dad to the stand.

"My son is an Eagle Scout," he testifies, then looking scornfully at me, he adds, "Up 'til this unfortunate event, my son has been as fine a boy as a dad could want."

The clerk reads into the record that Harry Roberts and Mark Berger are pleading guilty to conspiring to commit an act injurious to public health, a misdemeanor.

Harry is told to rise. He pleads guilty and admits to smoking pot once and assures the court, "Never again."

It's my turn. I plead guilty and declare, "I apologize for all the problems I've caused."

Judge Hyder sentences us to "11 months 29 days in jail, sentence suspended pending the recommendation of the Probation Department."

We entered the courthouse alone and leave alone. No one from our families accompanied us, nor have any of our Tennessee friends dared to show up. It's OK. I understand. We all have to move on. It's over.

We thank Lester profusely. He says, "You have a lovely lady here, now make her proud."

Deena and I exchange wordless hugs. Wiping the snow off the Chevy's windows and doors, we climb inside. The engine kicks over right away, for which I'm grateful. Glancing at the rearview mirror, Johnson City recedes into the distance. Driving conditions are dicey, so I stay on guard, mindful that under the beautiful snowy roads lies a layer of ice.

January 1968

POSTSCRIPT—NOW

The sun is beginning to rise as I walk onto the grounds of Brooklyn's Fort Hamilton Army Base. Two weeks ago, the infamous "Greetings" letter from the Selective Service System arrived ordering me to report today for induction into military service. Unlike the other inductees who are carrying small travel bags, my hands are empty. All I bring is the hope that being on probation will keep me out. Now, I worry that hope might not be enough.

Buses are lined up outside the induction center ready to transport the recruits to basic training. Once inside, I tell a sergeant there must be some mistake. He sends me to this office with a long wall of olive-green file cabinets and a wide linoleum counter of the same color. Signing the waiting list, I take a seat. A minute later this tough guy, hair greased back, white T-shirt with the sleeves rolled up, signs the list and sits down next to me.

"I ain't going," he says.

"No?"

"Bunch of pussies. Fuckin' army is run by pussies. Johnson's a commie, McNamara's a punk. They want the fuckin' gooks to win."

"They do?"

"Bomb 'em back to the Stone Age, like that general says. Nuke 'em, like we did the Japs. End of story. But no, these bitches just keep sending GI's over there to get their heads blown off. Me, I'm on bail for a weapons charge. I'll go to the pen before I'll go to Nam."

"Berger," a female voice calls.

I rise expecting to see a servicewoman, but instead it's this chick–a civilian, twenties, beehive hairdo, makeup just so, wearing a tight, V-neck sweater with a red, white, and green button that reads "Kiss Me I'm Italian." Since she's the only worker here, she may be all that stands between me and the swamps of Vietnam.

I tell her that I'm on probation and she goes to a file cabinet and retrieves my file card. "The Army knows you're on probation and is waiving it, you're cleared for induction."

I've less than a second, only a heartbeat, to respond before she moves on to the hoodlum. *Speak. Now.*

Holding her gaze, my words tumble out. "My probation officer gave me strict orders not to leave the state, if you put me on a bus, I'll be violating probation and be subject to arrest. Since you're the one sending me, you're an accessory and you could get in trouble too."

"In trouble too"—gets her attention. "Kiss-me" is wrestling with this one. Tapping my file card with her red polished nails, she looks up at the ceiling, then back at the card. The hard guy coughs. Taking out a red pen, she writes something on it, drops it in a wire basket, then, looking past me, she says, "Go home."

Heart fluttering, legs wobbly, I'm afraid to utter a sound. I turn and go out the door, down a long corridor toward the exit where a sentry is standing. My ears are peeled. *Is she going to reconsider and call out, "Soldier, stop that man"? What then?* Passing him, I nod slightly. No salute is necessary, I'm still a civilian.

Outside, I stride toward the main gate where two holstered MPs stand. *What if she phones them? Stop thinking, just keep going.* One of guards turns toward me and, again, I nod slightly, this time saying, "See you later," like I'm going out for a cup of coffee. He nods back. Maybe he thinks he knows me.

Now, I'm no longer on federal property. I'm in Bay Ridge, on 101st Street, by the water's edge. I march past the bus stop, one, two, three, four, past the subway at 96th Street and I keep going until I get to the 77th Street station. I stop and catch my breath. I did it. I wasn't inducted. The insanity of Vietnam can go on without me.

In our sunlit kitchen, Deena's eating breakfast. "That was quick and easy."

"Quick, yeah." Then I burst into tears and recount my experience as she holds me.

"I made it up. My probation officer never said nothing to me. All she had to do was call him and I'd either be headed to basic training or in handcuffs on the way to jail. I was lying to keep from dying."

Two weeks later, a letter arrives from the Selective Service reclassifying me as 1Y, a "temporarily unfit for service" designation, without the stigma of a 4F.

That night, in bed, I say, "It's crazy, but getting arrested in Tennessee just might have saved my life."

April 1968

Back to the Boro

PINK

"Like 'em?" Deena asks.

"They're very pink," I reply.

"Very, that's why I love 'em."

"What about the ones you have?"

"They're not pink."

"Other than that they're fine?"

"But, they're not pink."

"How much?"

"I knew you'd ask?"

"I kind of did too."

"I work, y'know."

"Me too."

"I put in my share."

"I put in everything."

"They're not returnable. Sometimes a girl just needs to get herself something pretty."

"Sometimes we have to pay the rent."

"Working in an office stinks. I want to learn a craft."

"Look, I'm almost finished with college, working just about full-time, but no complaints. After all that crap we went through in Tennessee—I was so down on myself, but no more. Let's just get through this, OK?"

"All I do is get on the subway, go to work, come home, eat, sleep, get on the subway, go to work . . . Thought pink eyeglasses would make me happy, maybe make you smile."

"If they could do that, I'd buy myself a pair."

January 1968

"Isn't Woodstock like an artists' colony?" asks Deena.

"For years and years. Lots of artists, writers, musicians—it's really hip."

"And Ezra's got a house there?"

"A weekend place, plus the apartment in Cobble Hill, plus his Brooklyn studio."

"Wow. He's must be loaded."

"Gallery shows here, in Europe. He's featured in a new book on psychedelic art."

"How'd you meet him?"

"Well, Spider knows this chick Elaine who knows Ezra. Like a year ago, she takes us up to his loft and we're floored by his paintings. They're unbelievable. We hang out and have a great time—talking about music, philosophy, telling stories—hilarious. A couple of weeks ago, I bump into him downtown and he asks me if I can help him prep a couple of big canvasses. Since I had a three-hour break between classes, I say sure. So, yesterday I prepped a couple of blank canvasses with gesso. No big deal, easy to do. As I'm leaving he goes, 'How 'bout you and your lady coming up to the country for the weekend? Hang out with Erica and me.' "

"Sounds *trés* cool. Erica's his wife, right? What's she like?"

"She's mother earth to his space cowboy."

The car ride's a pleasure—not much traffic, clear blue skies, and the Catskills are all dressed up in their prettiest greens. Once off the Thruway, we pass flowered fields, rocky streams, and farmhouses, a welcome change from Brooklyn. Seeing horses in a field, my wife says, "I always dreamed of owning one."

Stopping in town, we window shop on Tinker Street. Deena buys a red polka dot headband to go with her red sleeveless blouse. At the Elephant Café, we spot Van Morrison sitting with a group at a large round table in the corner, but it's cool. We do our thing, they do theirs.

Ten minutes outside of town, on a dirt road alongside a brook, is their white and green, clapboard country retreat. Erica welcomes us warmly. Ezra, curly haired, serious moustache, paint-stained white shirt, is in his studio, a large room that once served as the dining room.

His paintings fill every wall. His work is vibrantly colored, surreal, psychedelic. It's filled with waterfalls and shooting stars, flowers and moonbeams, angels and demons, earth and space—hundreds interwoven, swirling like a mandala—infused with luminescence, electricity, and atomic energy.

"Your art's so magical," says Deena.

"So's life, if you dig it."

"Nature from the inside," says his wife.

"You don't look at Ezra's paintings," I say. "You watch them."

"I feel like I'm taking a trip," says Deena.

"You are," says the artist.

Ezra answers the phone while Erica, pretty, tanned and trim, dressed in an orange tank top and white shorts, takes us to her herb garden. She's about my height which means she's taller than her husband.

"I'm studying homeopathic medicine," she says. "This garden's going to become our pharmacy."

Deena says, "I've been reading about that, it's fascinating. Can I ask, what's it like being married to such a great artist?"

"Ezra. He's a true artist, a visionary as well as a hipster and a chameleon all rolled into one."

Over a delicious vegetarian dinner, he regales us with stories. "Last summer, I hear Salvador Dali's in town, staying at the St. Regis. So I call my man Antonio who's got a van, and we load up one of my big paintings, drive up to the hotel. I go to the doorman, 'I got a painting for Mr. Dali.' So we get ushered into the King Cole Bar where the artist is sitting with two other people. Antonio and me set up the canvass against a wall, right across from him. Dali stands, studies the piece, and then he applauds. 'I love this. You must come see me tomorrow.'"

"So what'd he tell you?" asks Deena.

"Never went back. Why bother? Already got what I came for."

After dinner, our host says he has something special for dessert. Taking out an ornate, gold pill case, he unlatches it. Inside are several small purple pills.

Delicately holding one between his thumb and forefinger, he asks, "Know what this is?"

Placing one in my palm, I say, "Only by reputation. It's Owsley's, pure LSD."

"Give this man a silver dollar," says Ezra. "My friends in California introduced Owsley to my paintings and he sent these microgram-sized rocket ships to me with his blessings. Who wants to blast off?"

Deena's look says: *Did you know about this?* I shake my head no.

"You suggesting we all trip together?" I ask. Ezra just smiles.

While I've taken six or seven trips, Deena's taken only one. But given where we are, who we're with, and how we've both been longing to find a way to shed all the bad times of the past nine months, going with the flow feels like the way to go.

"Let's just take a half," Erica suggests. "That way, maybe, we'll get some sleep tonight."

Using an X-Acto knife, Ezra hands each of us each a piece.

"Mark, stay with me," Deena says.

"Positutely."

"OK, here goes."

We all walk into the living room where Erica starts doing simple yoga exercises. "Try them. They'll help you stay centered and calm."

Usually, there's a little interval before the liftoff, but not now. The four of us exchange self-conscious smiles. Deena pulls closer to me. Bach plays quietly on the stereo. I'm entranced by the music's majestic logic. Then it's the sounds of a sitar. Erica and Ezra chant quietly. I can't figure out how to speak. Deena's beside me, but she wiggling like a huge, red and blue caterpillar.

Poof. Time disappears. Dissolves. Gone. No such thing. Never was. Now. It's now now. Eternally now. Everything's phantasmagoric, magical, simultaneously familiar and bizarre. Swirling through worlds within hallucinatory worlds—hearing moonlight, tasting music, I see the energy that connects everything. Now riding a cresting ocean wave, now floating on a ripple in a river. *Stay cool. Been here before. Just let it wash over you. Don't resist. Relax. Let it carry you to the shore.*

When the surge of Owsley's elixir begins to subside, I smile at Deena. "You OK?"

"OK, OK."

"OK, OK, OK." We giggle.

She stretches a couple of times and then gets up. "I'm going to watch some paintings."

Ezra gets up and goes to his studio too. I'm drawn to the sounds of the brook. In the moonlight, it looks like a neon pulse, nature's synapse.

Deena and Ezra are talking and laughing quietly. I go outside and sit by the water. Erica comes and sits down alongside me. Glancing toward the house, she unclasps her hair, takes some cool spring water and wipes it over her face and arms and then, pulling back my hair, she gently wipes some on my neck and forehead.

Like two clouds magnetized, lightning passes between us. Our mouths, lips, and tongues enter into a sweet, soft, silent conversation. Our clothes are off so quickly, I wonder, were we naked to begin with? Cosmic question. As our bodies join in a dance, I'm at once attracted and repelled. One millisecond it's ecstasy and the next it's raw—like I've been cut with a razor. Pulling away, I say, "I need to check on Deena." Erica nods.

Stretched out on a chaise lounge, Ezra grins at me; I think: *What's funny?* Across the room, in a club chair, Deena's wrapped in a blue blanket with her legs pulled up to her chest. Has she been crying? She gives me a half-smile. I sit on the floor in front of her. Sliding down, she rests her head in my lap.

In a bit, Erica joins us. "I'll make some chamomile tea."

It's after two in the morning. Six hours have just evaporated. We sip the tea mostly in silence. Saying goodnight, we go to our room.

"You want to talk?" I ask.

"Tomorrow. Let's talk tomorrow."

After a fitful night, Deena says she wants to go home. I say sure. We tell our hosts we have stuff to do in the city. Saying goodbye, we exchange small hugs.

Halfway to Brooklyn, approaching the Tappan Zee Bridge, Deena says, "Let's get off and get something to eat."

Heading into Nyack, I find a diner. After we order pancakes, I say, "You can tell me."

"It was just a little too much for me," she says, then starts crying. "Mark, I'm sorry."

"It's all right, babe, it's all right."

June 1968

TURTLENECK

"You look cute in that turtleneck," Deena says.

"It's warm, really warm. What a great birthday present. Thanks for knitting it," I reply.

"Mom's so excited to be in her new apartment. After a million years, she's finally on her own."

"Your mom always live with your nana, even when she was married?"

"When my dad came home from the war, he moved in, only supposed to be temporary. Then my brother and me came along, and, then, my dad ran off with The Bimbo to Miami—left us flat cold. So, where could mom go? Sometimes temporary is permanent."

Our subway ride from Prospect Park to Brighton Beach takes 40 minutes, but all the Russian store signs make it feel like we've landed in the USSR. Just down the street from the boardwalk sits the tall, white apartment building that's my mother-in-law's new home.

Joe and Marsha, Deena's brother and sister in law, are already there.

"They call this Little Odessa," explains her mom. "This is where all the Soviet Jews are moving, 'cause it's near the water, like Odessa. It's like the second Exodus."

"What second?" I say, "The hundredth, at least."

"Commies are broke," Joe goes. "So they're selling off their Jews. Pay them $50,000 and get your Uncle Yakov on the next plane."

Looking around, Deena says, "Nice apartment."

We sit down for lunch.

"I went to the allergist this week for these blotches on my legs." Marsha says, pointing. "Turns out I'm allergic to nylon. Can you believe that?"

"You really suffer, don't you?" says my mother-in-law.

"I made a list of her allergies," Joe says.

"It's the accountant in him."

"Ten, Marsha's allergic to ten things."

"Ten so far, you mean."

"How's business?" Deena asks.

"They're making me comptroller—youngest comptroller in the company's history."

"How old's the company?" I ask.

"Don't matter, I'm the youngest."

I eat in no time. "I've got a paper due on Monday, so I have to go. Deena, why don't you stay?"

Once outside, I pull off the turtleneck. It's suffocating me.

February 1969

VALENTINE'S DAY

"A Valentine's Day party?" asks Deena. "Thought on Valentine's Day, it's supposed to be just the two of us, with you giving me chocolates and a cute present, and then, who knows, maybe some horizontal dancing?"

"Hank's friend Reggie's having the party because it's his girlfriend Bianca's birthday, and because it's the weekend, not because it's Valentine's Day. The guys I know all feel like me— that Hallmark, manufactured, romantic crap is nauseating. How 'bout I get you a box of chocolates somewhere?"

"Wow. I'm thrilled. It's just that the girls in the office were all gushing about the nice places their guys are taking them to tonight."

"Yeah, well, everyone you work with is super straight."

Because the party is up near the George Washington Bridge, we decide to drive. That way we won't have to deal with the subways late at night.

Around ten friends and acquaintances are already there, including Hank. Since he graduated from Buffalo, we've renewed our friendship. With beer and wine in the fridge, chips and salsa on the table, and some joints being passed around, it's pretty mellow. On the stereo, Otis is singing about sitting on that dock.

Deena starts talking with Bianca, the birthday girl, while I go into the bedroom with Hank who pulls out a pint of Calvert's soft whiskey. We toast the night.

The phone rings and it's Becky, Hank's lady, calling to say she's lost—took the wrong train. She's at a laundromat in Washington Heights, about a mile away. Of course, there are no cabs to be found.

I say to Hank, "I got my car, we can go pick her up."

I tell Deena that Hank and I are going to pick up Becky. As we're almost out of the door, Reggie says, "How 'bout picking up some more beer and chips?"

"No problem," I say, "I can cover it." I reach into my pants pocket to check how much money I have in my wallet. Out come my keys, a lighter and a pack of rolling papers, but that's all. I mutter, "Where's my wallet?"

"You don't have your wallet?" asks Deena.

"Must have left it on the kitchen table. Can you give me some money?"

"I'm coming, too," she says.

I want to say don't bother, but her look tells me otherwise. Once the three of us are outside, she says, "You can't drive."

"Sure I can. I hardly had anything," I say, leaving out what Hank and I were just doing.

"No, you can't drive, because you don't have your driver's license."

"It's just a couple of blocks, no big deal."

Hank walks down the street, leaving us alone to work this out.

"You can't drive," Deena insists again, "Because if you get stopped, the cops could bust you for driving without a license and if they find out you're on probation, who knows what'll happen."

"And how are they supposed to find out?" I demand.

"They just might."

"What, would you tell them?"

"I won't have to tell them, because I'm telling you, you're not driving."

I glance at Hank, remembering that time when I told him "listen to me and do what I say," and he did. Now here I am and Deena's basically saying the same thing to me. I hate it. I know she's right, and I hate her for it. All the bad stuff we've been through engulfs me. I want to grab her and shake her.

"Becky's waiting," Deena says. "Give me the keys, please."

"Here's the fuckin' keys," I say, throwing them at her, hitting her in the shoulder.

As soon as I do it, I regret it. I apologize, but it's too late. She almost starts crying, but pulls back, she's not going to give me the satisfaction.

I let Hank sit up front and I climb into the backseat. I never thought I would act like that toward Deena.

We pick up Becky and I get back up front. When Deena pulls up to Reggie's, they get out, we say "later" and keep on going. All the way back to Brooklyn, I try to come up with something to say, but I can't.

I open our apartment door. Deena immediately goes into the bathroom. She's there for a while. I sit on the couch, not knowing what to expect. When she emerges, she looks me right in the eye and says, "This is one Valentine's Day I'll never forget."

February 1969

"Was that good for you?" I ask.

"Are you kidding? I think we woke up the neighbors."

"I love you."

"Me, too."

"I'm sorry for the mix up."

"I guess you didn't hear me say we were meeting my mom at six."

"I thought you said seven."

"We were just worried something happened to you."

"That's why you were both screaming at me?"

"We were upset."

"Listen, I can take care of myself."

"Y'know, sometimes you think you can take better care of yourself than you actually do."

"Huh?"

"Howie and Stacy, your new college buddies, they're trouble."

"All my old friends split for the coast. So I'm hanging with these guys, they're cool."

"They're weird."

"Let's stay on us," I say.

"OK. Seems like the only time we make love is after a fight."

"Make-up sex."

"Since Tennessee, things have been tough. We had a cool life there. I'm tired of the city," Deena says.

"What can I say? I'm not quitting college, made a promise to myself and I'm not breaking it."

"It's just been rough."

"Maybe if we made love more, things wouldn't seem so complicated."

"Yeah, I know."

"That was nice."

"Dynamite."

March 1969

SEVENS

After a rainy week, April is finally giving it all it's got. Skies are sunny, temps are rising, and the breeze is just right. But I'm experiencing a bit of bad weather, because Deena is going away for the weekend. Pecking me on the check, she says, "See you Sunday night. Please meet me at the bus."

"I'll be there." I say, pecking her back. "Say hi to Lance and his old lady. Hey, we're finally gonna to find out if Virginia Beach is as hip as they say."

"They've been having problems. Lance told Gwen about the rap sessions we have and she wants me to come down and show them how they work. That way they can get everything out in the open."

"Yeah, I know. Hope it helps. Meanwhile, I'll work on my term papers. Have fun for both of us."

Next morning, my mother-in-law calls. "Deena there?"

"Nah, she's away for the weekend. Didn't she tell you?"

"Tell me? When does she ever tell me anything?"

"She's in Virginia visiting our friends Lance and Gwen. I'm swamped with school work, so I stayed home."

"Oh, I see. . . . Well, tell her I called."

Oh, I see? What does she see? Who cares? I've got two papers to knock out in four days, one on Jean Genet, the self-acknowledged thief who became a celebrated avant-garde French playwright, and the other on John Dewey, the big daddy of American education.

Seven weeks from now, after seven years in four different colleges, I'm finally going to be a college graduate. I've written so many papers on so many different topics that I think, maybe, I should publish them as *Mark Berger's Collected Term Papers*.

I work hard all weekend—reading, writing, and rewriting. By Sunday night, my head's abuzz, but the end is in sight. Taking the subway to the Port Authority terminal in Times Square, I watch Deena emerge from the bus, looking good in jeans and a scooped-neck, tie dyed T-shirt.

"How'd it go?"

"Gwen's family's gigantically furious with her for shacking up with Lance, so she's pushing for marriage."

"And Lance?"

"Lance is Lance. He's putting together a new band, working in a leather shop. There's a good chance the owners will ask him to run their other shop in Nag's Head."

"How'd the rap session go?"

"Nowhere fast. But we did go to this cool club, Rogues. Their friends were playing. They sound like the Yardbirds."

A couple of Fridays later, Deena tells me, "I've got to go back to Virginia Beach."

"Huh?"

"Look, you're always so busy. I'm tired of just sitting around doing nothing?"

"Nothing? There's tons to do here. How come you're just telling me about it now?"

"What? So we can have a fight? It's just for two days."

"Call your mom. I don't want to have to deal with her."

"Meet me at the bus, please."

Sunday night, getting off the Greyhound, Deena barely kisses me. Long trip, maybe she's tired.

On the A train, my mind's racing faster than the express. I keep hearing her mother say, "Oh, I see."

While Deena unpacks, I make a pot of mint tea. I light a cigarette, stub it out, light another. Deena pours her tea and sits across from me.

Trying to hold in the question I dread asking, it spits itself out. "Gwen wasn't there, right?"

Deena looks away. "She had to go home."

"Deena, don't do this. You knew she wasn't going to be there?"

Deena eyes tear up as do mine.

My voice cracks, "You know me, I won't live a lie."

"Lance was so down."

"Consoling him? Is that what you call it?"

"He's my friend."

"The motherfucker used to be mine too. Bet the two of you are much closer now. When did this start? Back in Tennessee? How am I supposed to sleep next to you?"

"I don't know. Things haven't been good between us."

"It's been hard. Our lives got set back, but I keep thinking we're just about through it, right? I keep saying to myself . . ."

"I hate it here. Brooklyn sucks. I don't want to be a teacher's wife. I need to be somewhere else, somewhere more peaceful."

". . . if we just stick together. Deena, I love you."

I start sobbing uncontrollably. I feel like a wounded animal. Deena is crying too. What hurts the most is that neither of us can turn to the other for consolation. Our bonds of trust have been shattered. We've reached this crossroad together, but now she's leaving me, and there's nothing I can do. Swallowing my tears, coughing, swallowing them again, I summon all my strength.

"How long will it take you to be out of here?"

"Couple of weeks."

"No, that'll kill me—seven days, one week. That's all I can give you. Don't drag this out and drag me down."

"I'm sorry."

"Sorry? That's all you can say? You just broke my heart."

April 1969

END OF MAY

I know this Memorial Day weekend will be a memorable one. On my kitchen table, arranged in an arc before me, are my textbooks, class notes, index cards, legal pads, pens, a pack of Camels, a red ashtray, a mug of coffee, and a vial of uppers.

Sixty-two hours from now, on Monday at 8 a.m. sharp, I have the first of my two final finals, followed, at 10, by the last one, my final final. They are the only requirements left for my college degree. Seven long years of failures, false starts, restarts, detours, and persistence have gotten me to this point. My weekend plans are simple: cram, study, cram.

The sky is turning from blue to charcoal. Black clouds ride low on the horizon. Thunder and lightning are heading this way. Stormy weather, yeah, I know about that.

My emotions are a roller coaster. I can't get through a night without getting wakened by nightmares. Even my daydreams are filled with agonizing flashbacks. Deena's gone. Been gone a month. Gone south, like our marriage. Parachuting out of our life together, she landed with Lance in Virginia Beach—our good buddy Lance. The fuckin' bastard. Whatever happy memories I had of our life together have been shot to hell.

I keep wondering if we could have made it through the maze of uncertainty and despair that engulfed our lives after we got arrested in Tennessee—charged with felony drug possession, staring at mandatory sentences of three years in a state penitentiary. Incredibly, our attorney, Lester Clayter, worked out a plea bargain with me getting a year's probation and the charges against Deena dropped. While the legal outcome was all we could have hoped for, the ordeal scarred our relationship.

I resumed my plan to become a teacher by re-enrolling in Long Island University and taking extra credits to graduate as quickly as possible. Deena got an office gig. She hated it, but once I was working, my income would support us while she learned a craft. I went along blithely thinking things were solid when they were actually no more substantial than the sand mandalas Buddhist monks fashion.

Deena told me she couldn't take Brooklyn anymore. But, for me, it's is the only place I feel safe. It's a mystery how I've managed to keep myself together these past four weeks. Who says man can't live on cigarettes, coffee, reefer, cheap wine, and sandwiches?

Then there's my parents. Ten days after the arrest, on our way to my parents' apartment to talk things over, I tell Deena, "It'll be tough, but doable. They already know I smoke pot, so, it's not like they're finding out about it for the first time."

But as soon as we sit down, my mom starts screaming at me, "So, now you're a junkie."

"Junkie? I'm no junkie." I say. "Like I told you, what, three years ago, once in a while I smoke pot."

With that my dad stands up, "Listen here, sonny, if you want to learn something, sit down and shut up."

So, of course, I get up, grab Deena, and as we split, I yell, "Talking to you is useless. Just leave me alone." That was 18 months ago.

Put it away. It's done. It's history. Pouring a glass of water, I take out an upper. I know I swore before Judge Hyder I'd stay clean. But I meant clean in Tennessee. That promise I'll keep. I'm sure no one there gives a damn what I do here. Swallowing the pill, I think, *I'm just a stranger in this world.*

First up is biology—all facts, all the time. Using index cards and legal pads, I start winnowing down what I need to know. My mind is like a shelf in a grocery store that I'm packing with cans filled with facts about the kingdom, phylum, class, order, family, genus, and species of all living things. I plan to keep stuffing that information into my brain until there's no room left.

Friday evening into Saturday morning, I read and write until I have several hundred cards and 20 pages of handwritten notes. Now, all I have to do is memorize everything and know it cold.

Showering and eating a bit, I reset the table for my final on Shakespeare. Big Will's storytelling and dialogue are dazzling—so lithe and taut, simple and complicated, ridiculous and profound. There's nothing he can't do with words.

Some of my classmates have the chutzpah to criticize the world's greatest playwright. These geniuses point out things they think Shakespeare must have missed. They complain his plots involve too much miscommunication, misassumptions, and venality. But I know the Bard knows. His tragedies are primal, they pierce my heart. Rereading *Othello*, my eyes are so filled with tears. I can barely see the words.

So I go from biology to Shakespeare and back again. Early Sunday, after crashing for two hours, I take a walk by the lake in Prospect Park. By afternoon, I stop taking speed. By two Monday morning, my head's spinning. I'm exhausted but satisfied. I've gone through everything and have learned as much as I possibly can. Time to catch some rest.

Life's challenging me to a battle. Will I survive? Might I thrive? Biology at 8, Shakespeare at 10, I'll know at noon.

May 1969

MR. MCCOY

As our final semester winds down, a classmate asks Dr. Moore, our education professor, to talk about getting a teaching job in the fall.

Dr. Moore explains, "Ed. majors can either wait for the Board of Education to assign them or seek jobs on their own. Waiting for the Board to act will result in an assignment to a 'rough and tough' school, because that's where most of the openings exist. Positions in good schools are mostly filled through word of mouth or connections."

I raise my hand, "What about non-education majors?"

He replies, "Those individuals have to find teaching positions on their own. My advice is don't delay; start looking immediately."

"What about Ocean Hill-Brownsville?" my friend Barry Cohen asks.

"Let me be honest. Few future educators would want to work in a district that is run by the radical militants who caused the horrendous citywide school strike back in the fall."

I smile to myself—that's exactly where I want to teach.

After class, three of us go to the College Donut Shop across Flatbush Avenue.

Connie Vincent, in her LIU sweatshirt, says, "My mother's friend is an assistant principal in Bensonhurst and she's promised me an interview at her school."

"I've got a provisional license." says Barry Cohen, in a Cornell T-shirt. "I need a job, because I need a draft deferral. Any school is better than going to Vietnam, but I don't have any idea where to start?"

"I do," I say, "Ocean Hill-Brownsville."

"Are you crazy?" asks Connie. "Didn't you hear Professor Moore?"

"That's his opinion," I say. "I followed what happened with the teachers strike and I definitely support Ocean Hill over the teachers union and the Board of Education."

"So, you're a militant." she says, nudging me with her elbow.

"Look, the Board of Education has been failing blacks and other minorities forever. Can you imagine being a parent sending your child to one of those schools knowing full well that they're the worst in the city? And, after decades of failure, what has the education establishment done to improve their track record? Nothing, *nada*, *bupkis*."

"Hold on." says Connie. "Too many of those kids come to school unprepared. Whose fault it that?"

"Mark's saying, it's a vicious cycle," says Barry.

I say, "Last year the Ford Foundation came up with a new approach. With permission from the central board and the state, they funded a couple of 'demonstration districts.'"

"Yeah, they demonstrated how to shut down all the schools in the city," says Connie.

"The Foundation asked: Would education improve if the residents elected their own school boards, like people do on Long Island? They reasoned that working together, community reps and educators might come up with ways to improve their schools."

"But if that district superintendent, y'know, the guy with the pipe, Rhody McCoy, hadn't fired all those teachers, the union wouldn't have gone on strike," says Barry.

I shake my head. "That, my friends, is the big lie. The lie Al Shanker, the union chief, told over and over again, and the newspapers and television stations lapped it up. But that's not what went down. All McCoy did was to tell 13 teachers and six administrators that the district wasn't going to rehire them in the fall and that they should report back to the central board for reassignment. McCoy never fired anyone."

"I've never heard of a teacher being fired," says Barry.

"They all could have been reassigned in a day. McCoy was trying to do his job—move out bad teachers and move in good ones. Professor Moore calls it radical, but on Long Island, they call it common sense. Education 101: Students learn better with better teachers."

"How you explain it makes sense," says Barry.

"Everyone talks about making the world better, I can't think of a better way for me to do that than becoming a teacher, the kind who really wants to make a difference."

Walking back to campus, Barry asks me when I plan to contact Ocean Hill-Brownsville. I tell him I already have and they told me to call right after graduation.

~

A day after our commencement, Barry and I are sitting in the reception area of the Ocean Hill-Brownsville Demonstration District. The door to the inner office opens and there he is, the controversial school superintended of the Ocean Hill-Brownsville district, Mr. Rhody McCoy—taller and thinner than he appears on camera, wearing a tan blazer, white shirt, green striped tie and smoking a meerschaum pipe.

Introducing himself, he escorts us into his office. "Gentlemen, thank you for coming. I understand you're both looking for elementary school teaching positions."

Barry says, "Yes, yes we are."

"Good. Were you education majors?"

"I wasn't," I say.

"Neither was I," Barry says.

"Then, you're the kind of candidates we're looking for."

"Great," Barry says with a smile.

Mr. McCoy continues, "I say that with regret. I wish education departments offered courses that really prepared future teachers to educate less-fortunate students. The model they use is that of a middle-class youngster with an intact two-parent family. That's not what we have here. We need to develop a new approach to education that meets our students where they are."

"I believe in student-centered classrooms," I say. "Being a teacher means knowing and respecting your students."

"I like your enthusiasm," say Mr. McCoy.

"I believe in community control, so does Barry. And, I definitely don't believe teachers should strike and shut down the schools. The kids have it hard enough already."

"Today's kids are tomorrow's adults," says Barry, "So whatever we do will have a big impact on their lives."

Mr. McCoy says, "Please tell me a little about yourselves."

Barry says, "I've worked as a day camp counselor and I really enjoy working with younger children."

I'm next. "Last year, at the LIU tutoring clinic, I worked with a third grader named Elijah, and he really did great. I loved being able to help him. Also, a couple of years ago, I worked for Major Owens, when he ran for city council on the Brooklyn Freedom Democratic line. Although he lost that election, he wasn't defeated. Last year, the mayor appointed him to head the city's anti-poverty program."

"I know him well. He's a good man," says Mr. McCoy. "All right, gentlemen, I'm convinced. I have a school in mind, P.S. 73, but you'll have to persuade the principal, Mr. Grimaldi, to give you a chance. I'll call him to let him know you're on your way."

The drive over in a gypsy cab reveals a neighborhood that's filled with empty tenements, dirty streets, and few stores. At the school, we sit in the main office for an hour, while a constant stream of people enter and leave the principal's office. Finally, the secretary waves us in.

Mr. Grimaldi, in his fifties, with a paunch, is matter of fact. "You both made a good impression on Mr. McCoy. I don't have time to interview you, so instead I have a proposal—if you substitute teach here for the rest June, and you do a good job, I'll hire you for September. Fair enough?"

"Start teaching now?" asks Barry.

"College is over, right?" says the principal.

"I'll do it," I say.

"Me, too," adds Barry.

"Good. See Mrs. T., the school secretary. She'll set you up."

While we fill out forms and give her our licenses, Mrs. T. asks, "Did Mr. Grimaldi tell you about the school?"

"He said if we did a good job subbing," Barry says, "he'll hire us for September."

"Trial by fire. No matter," she says. "If I know about a teacher absence in advance, you'll get a call the night before, but don't be surprised to hear your phone ring at 6:30 in the morning asking you to come in. Make sure you get here by 8:40. Can you do that?"

"We have to, so sure." I say.

On the subway, Barry says, "You were right. McCoy's a gentleman, he's nothing like the way he's portrayed in the news. I mean he hired the two of us, two white, Jewish cats, without a blink."

"Like I told you, he's not a racist, he's sincere about changing the schools."

"Mark, tell me the truth, do you think we're going to be OK?"

"We got jobs, didn't we? The rest is up to us."

June 1969

Going North

BUGS AND SPARROWS

"Bugs are good, Volvos and Saabs, too, they all pick up hitchhikers." My well-traveled friend, Bennett, advises me. "But watch out for the Man. Travel clean and thumb rides at on-ramps, not on highways. Don't ride with drunks—if they pick you up, bail as fast as you can. Tell them anything, they're drunk, what do they care? But bail. A sure thing—a freak driving a VW bus."

Attempting my first trip via thumb, I'm at the entrance to the Prospect Expressway, a mile from my apartment, when a long-haired freak in a sky-blue VW bus pulls over to give me a ride, I think of Bennett and smile.

"I'm headed to Vermont," I say.

"Goin' to Liberty. I can drop you at the Thruway/Route 17 split. Jump in."

"Cool."

Sliding my backpack and sleeping bag into the back, I climb up front. Introducing myself, "I'm traveling to the Bennington Craft Fair for the weekend, planning on meeting up with two of my friends from Tennessee, who'll be there selling their pottery and weavings."

His name's Jason and he's on his way to see his girlfriend who's working in a camp in the Catskills. The vibe between us is solid. It feels like we're old friends meeting up for the first time. The radio is tuned to WNEW-FM and we nod along to the Who's "My Generation."

Pete Fornatale, the DJ says, "It looks like that Woodstock Music Festival is gonna happen. Talk about 'hippie heaven.'"

Turning to Jason, I say "I don't know about you, but I hate the term hippie."

"Me too," he replies. "The straights made the word up to make it seem like all we're about is sex, y'know, using our hips."

"Yeah, that way they can pretend their lifestyle actually makes sense. Except it doesn't. Everywhere I turn, it's bullshit. They talk peace, but they practice war, just look at Nam."

"Yeah, forget love, let's hate everyone who isn't like us."

"What about freedom? Try to be free and they shut you down quick," I say.

"Tell me about it."

"To me, we're freaks, pure and simple. We don't want to dress like them, think like them, live like them."

"I dig that. We're trying to get to the next level of evolution," Jason adds.

"Inner space explorers. If we all pull together, maybe we can get there."

"Freaks."

"Freaks."

We both nod.

Two more hitches and five hours later, I'm on Route 7 outside of Albany. Forty minutes pass before a tan bug comes into view. The driver, wearing a beard and a Red Sox cap, pulls over. When I tell him where I'm headed, he says, "Welcome aboard."

Riding shotgun is this adorable chick—long, red hair flowing over a skimpy white peasant blouse and a smile that could melt a glacier or, in my case, a frozen heart. Man, I haven't felt stirrings like these in a long time, not since Deena split on me.

He's Fred, she's Rosie. They go to Cornell.

"We're doing a weekend hike on the Appalachian Trail," Rosie says.

Leaning forward between the front seats, I go, "I can't figure out hiking. You get on this trail that's lined with trees and grass and stuff, and you trudge and trudge until you end up at a place that's lined with trees and grass and stuff."

Rosie's grinning. Fred says, "There's flora and fauna."

"So instead of working so hard to end up kind of where I began, I'd rather just hang out, smoke a joint and dig the sky."

"We love Vermont," Fred says.

"Ask me, the first Vermonters weren't too sharp."

"No?"

"Dig this, in French, *vert* means green and *mont* means mountain, right? Ver-mont is how the French say green mountain."

"Yeah, so?"

"Here's the thing. Y'know the state's nickname? It's the 'Green Mountain State.' The state's nickname is the same as their name. It's like saying 'My name's Mark, but everyone calls me Mark.' That's the best those people could come up with. Like I said, not too sharp."

Rosie laughs and laughs.

We roll into Bennington. I spot an ice cream shop and insist on buying us all a cone. They drive me up the hill to the high school where the craft fair is taking place and we say goodbye.

It's late in the afternoon. The exhibition hall is quiet. Not many presenters are left and fewer shoppers. I pick up a site map to locate Izzy and Norma's booth. On my way, I notice colorful signs for the various craft enterprises, like Curiouser Candles and Red Dragon Silk Works.

When I locate my friends' booth, all that's there is their sign and a folding table. I look for a note addressed to me, but find none. A couple of booths over a guy is packing up his stained-glass panels. I introduce myself and ask whether he might have heard where the potter and weaver went. He just shakes his head and continues working. Talk about a bummer. My only plan was to meet them. Now what?

Wandering around trying to figure out what to do, I pass a booth with a banner that reads: "Sparrow Leather." Underneath is a biblical quotation I first heard in Tennessee: "His eye is on the sparrow."

At the Bennington Potters display, two guys in paisley bandanas are packing up crates, so I make my way over to them.

"Hi, I'm Mark, just hitchhiked up from Brooklyn."

"I'm Jeff," says the taller of the two, "and this is Lloyd. Looks like the fair is over for the day."

"Came here to meet up with a couple of my friends from Tennessee. Izzy's a potter, like you cats, and his wife Norma's a weaver. But all that's left at their booth is a table. I've no idea where they're staying. So I thought maybe you dudes might know of a place where I could crash?"

"Give us a second."

They step away from the booth and talk quietly. I hear Lloyd say, "What the hell?" and see Jeff nod.

When they return, Lloyd says, "We got a small farmhouse. You OK with sleeping outside?"

"The earth below, the sky above. I'm totally cool with that."

I help them carry crates outside to their pickup truck. When we're done, I hop in back, settling down among the boxes and display racks.

An hour or so later, I'm in an old-fashioned kitchen eating a bowl of chili and vegetables with Jeff and Lloyd and their roommates, Emmy and Gabrielle, and we're all laughing at something Emmy just said. Taking a deep breath, I think: Bennett was right about the bugs; maybe that sign about the sparrow was right too.

July 1969

STEPS

On Sunday, instead of returning to the craft fair with Lloyd and Jeff, I decide to stay at the farmhouse. Going on a walk in the nearby field with Emmy and Gabrielle, I learn that both girls attend Bennington College, where Gabrielle, who's from Manhattan, is majoring in French lit, and Emmy, who's from Detroit, is studying dance.

"I've always wondered how dancers handle being so close to each other." I say to Emmy.

She goes, "You have to learn to separate physical intimacy from emotional intimacy."

"That's most of French literature in a sentence," Gabrielle says.

"I dig jazz. But, I don't get modern dance."

"Jazz tells stories with sound, dance does it with movement," says Emmy. "It takes time to understand it. Y'know what, in two weeks I'll be performing at the American Dance Festival at Connecticut College. If you're interested in going, I probably could get you a ticket and a place to stay in the dorm."

"Really? You'd do all that for me?"

"It's not that much. My mom's a choreographer, so I've been going there forever. I know everyone. It'd be nice to have a friend along."

"If you can arrange it, I'll be there."

Two weeks later, as I wait outside the dorm to meet Emmy, I watch small groups of dancers pass by. What strikes me is how they all walk erect and seem to flow as they move. The guys are built like fire hydrants, solid from the waist up and the girls' bodies are toned and their legs muscular. I notice as they go along, some of the guys casually brush and touch their friends, in the way lovers do. I know guys who go for guys, but they keep it hush-hush. Here, it's just about out in the open. For them, the festival must be like stepping into a different world, one that gives them the freedom to be who they are.

Emmy appears and takes me to my small dorm room where I drop off my backpack. Because she needs to eat something before tonight's performance, she leads me to the cafeteria. On the way she says, "My mom's joining us. She wants to meet you."

"Me? Doesn't she have better things to do?"

"She loves meeting my friends."

Emmy's mother, like her daughter, is tall and athletic, but where Emmy has smile lines, her mom has worry lines. "Hi, I'm Ruth," she says, extending her hand, "Emmy's told me a little bit about you: a Brooklynite who's going to become a teacher. Is that what your parents do?"

I get it. She thinks I'm seeing her daughter, so she's conducting The Interview. But since I'm not, I don't feel like I have to go through the application process. Avoiding her question, I ask, "Is your group ready for tonight's performance?"

"One last rehearsal and then we'll find out," Ruth says.

"Mom, too many rehearsals dull the dancer."

Her mom turns and faces the windows. "I love the arboretum here. It contains over a thousand varieties of trees. All trees need strong roots to thrive or they wither and die, like tumbleweeds." Now, turning to face us both, she adds, "Tumbleweeds are barely worth our attention. Staying rooted keeps you strong." And with that, she gathers her belongings and says, "I have to go. Nice meeting you."

"That was heavy," I say.

"My mom always wanted me to follow in her footsteps. When I accepted the offer to go to college in Vermont, it was a shocker. Now she's afraid I might abandon dance altogether. Getting out of her gravitational pull has made me aware of my own."

"Gravitational pull, that reminds me. Did you know the moon walk is tonight? I can't wait to see it. It'll be incredible."

"Getting my dance routine right is enough incredible for me."

The auditorium is mostly full and the audience is enthusiastic. The first dance is furious and confusing with the dancers frequently stopping and staring at the audience. The next troupe dances to the sounds of dolphin calls, the dancers look like they're swimming across the stage. Emmy's group performs last. Four women and two men perform what looks like a modern square dance. It's fun to watch and looks like fun to do. When they finish, Ruth comes onstage for a round of applause and a young dancer presents her with a bouquet of roses.

Afterwards, Emmy and I go to the dorm lounge which is filled with her fellow performers. Thankfully, I haven't missed the moon walk, it's due to happen within an hour.

I turn to a male dancer from Emmy's group. "You all dance like you're walking on air."

He says, "Thanks. Like Ruth says: Great dancers are the ones who seem to defy gravity."

In the background I can hear someone griping about the space program, "Think of all the schools and hospitals that could be built with the money this moon mission cost."

I restrain myself from saying: "Get real, you are about to witness one of mankind's greatest accomplishments."

The lunar module door opens, Neil Armstrong takes several steps down the ladder, hesitates for a moment, and then hops onto the moon's surface.

"That's one small step for man, one giant leap for mankind."

Spontaneous cheering erupts throughout the lounge.

Later, as I stroll with Emmy back to her dorm, she says, "Mark, I've been thinking about what I want to do with my life and where dance fits in. I've decided that when I get back to school, I'm going to change my major."

"What did the astronaut say? His small step is a giant leap. No matter what you decide, I'm sure you'll land on your feet."

Looking up at the crescent moon, Emmy says, "How extraordinary. They're up there right now."

July 1969

Bennett, my apartment house neighbor, asks me, "You got any plans for next week?"

"I'm living existentially."

"So you don't have any. My cousin Laura and me are going to Montreal to stay overnight with a friend of hers and then to Toronto to visit a cousin of ours. Want to come along?"

"I'm down for that."

A week later, we pull up to Laura's friend's house in a high-class Montreal neighborhood called Mont Royal. Laura and Antoinette became friends years ago when they both were campers at a sleepaway camp in the Adirondacks and have remained close ever since.

When the girls see each other they smile so much their cheeks must hurt. They're dressed the same—both wearing bell-bottomed jeans, beaded bracelets, sandals, and halter tops. We're led downstairs to a finished basement, which is decorated with Montreal Canadiens memorabilia. Sitting on the floor are four of her friends listening to the Beatles' *Revolver* album.

Checking them out, I wonder what a hip Brooklyn cat like me could have in common with these kids. This guy passes me a bottle of wine and his friend comes over and sits down. The three of us get to talking and it turns out we dig the same music—Miles Davis and Muddy Waters and we're deep into the same writers—Hesse and Kafka. Victor is big, with a head of bushy hair and a beard to match, His best friend, Andre, is about my height, bright blue eyes behind horn-rimmed glasses, and wearing chinos and a knit shirt.

As they leave, Victor hands me his phone number. "Call me if you decide to stay in town."

In the morning, I decide I'd rather check out Montreal than go to Toronto, so I call Victor. "Man, I'd love to stay in Montreal, but I need a place to crash."

"My parents are away so you can stay here for now."

I tell Bennett and Laura about my change of plans and they're fine with it.

That evening, their friend Ellen joins Victor, Andre, Antoinette, and me. She's got hair to her waist and is pencil thin. After we pass around a joint. Antoinette says, "Let's go somewhere. Didn't we promise Harvey we'd visit him?"

Andre tells me that Harvey is an American ex-pat, a draft dodger, whose name isn't really Harvey. He lives an hour away with his Canadian girlfriend.

"He's so hip," Victor says. "He turned us on to Lightning Hopkins. Aye, let's go."

In no time we're outside the city limits, with Victor piloting his family's Peugeot down a dark, two lane highway. Antoinette's up front, along with Ellen who's using a flashlight to read a map.

"Is it Millersville or Millerton?" Ellen asks.

Antoinette says, "I never know one from the other."

"That's because they're exactly the same, but in two different locations," says Victor.

"Like parallel universes," Andre adds. "Let's find a phone and call him?"

"Why didn't we think of that before," says Victor.

"He doesn't have one," says Antoinette. "He's convinced the FBI would tap his line."

"In Canada?" I ask.

"Why not?"

Ellen says, "Millerton's closer."

"Closer is better," Victor says.

Knowing where Harvey lives is better, I think, but I remind myself I'm just along for the ride. I start dozing off, when I hear retching sounds coming from up front.

"Stop the car," Antoinette yells. "Ellen has to throw up."

Making a quick turn at a four-way flashing red light, Victor pulls onto the shoulder. Ellen jumps out and proceeds to heave, catch her breath, and then do it again. After about ten minutes she says, "I'm all right now."

"What time is it?" I ask.

"Eleven twenty," Victor says. "Is Harvey even awake?"

"How should I know?" says Andre, "We can't call him, eh, and, it seems like we don't know where he lives."

"Exactly," Ellen says and everyone just cracks up.

Just then a white, Ford Econoline van, with "The Friers" hand-stenciled on its side, stops at the flashing light, and, seeing us, pulls onto the opposite shoulder. The side door slides open, rock music blasts out, and a fat guy in a monk's cassock and a skinny girl in a pink T-shirt, crinoline petticoat, and pink tights stumble out.

"Need some help?" the monk asks.

"We're OK," Victor replies. "Ellen here got car sick is all."

"Where we are?" Antoinette asks,

"Hinton."

Taking the map and flashlight, Antoinette says, "Yes, I see."

"Is there a petrol station nearby, we're getting low," says Victor.

"All the stations around here are closed," says the monk.

Now three other guys and another girl climb out of the van. The guys are in monks' garb, including those little beanies. The new girl has on a Poodle skirt and saddle shoes from the '50s.

"Don't want to pry," says Andre, "but I didn't think monks could be with chicks."

"We're the Friers," the fat monk says. "That's our band's name. We're coming from a gig."

"Yeah, to blow everyone's mind, they dress like friars," says the petticoated girl. "But our name is spelled with an 'e.' "

"Like beetles and the Beatles," I note, apparently to no one.

The leader says, "We got a big old house in the next town. You could stay with us tonight."

"Cool," says Victor.

"The coolest," says Antoinette.

"Get 'em while they're hot," Ellen mumbles, smiling at the musicians.

Arriving at their house, they set up and play us a couple of their songs. The fat guy is their lead guitarist and singer, the driver is their drummer, the two others are on rhythm guitar and bass, while the chicks sing back-up. Their best song is "Honey Girl," which they pray will make them famous.

"You guys could be the new Guess Who," says Victor.

Antoinette secures a small bedroom for her and Victor. Ellen and the drummer mosey upstairs. Andre grabs the couch, I find some blankets and spread them on a foam rubber mat.

Before falling asleep, I think about the past two days. I'm staying with Victor, a guy I just met, and he and his friends have taken me into their circle, no questions asked. And, now, in the middle of the night, a rock band stopped to help us out and invited the five of us to be overnight guests in their home, again, no questions asked. That's the thing about the counterculture, from sharing a joint to passing a bottle of wine to picking up hitchhikers to sharing our homes—in no time flat, we've developed a culture of generosity. Can I imagine my parents or anyone from that generation ever extending themselves the way we freaks regularly do for each other? Never, not in a million years.

In the morning, as we're piling into the car, Victor says to me, "Even in Canada, adventure is just around a corner."

"And so are our brothers and sisters."

July 1969

A couple of mornings later, Victor's parents call to say they're coming home.

"Is there somewhere else I can stay?"

"Let's ask Andre."

Meeting at the Yellow Door, a bar near McGill University, Victor asks Andre if I can stay at his house.

Andre agrees, with a proviso. "My dad and mom are away for the weekend, but we have to be careful not disturb my *grand-mère*. She lives with us."

"*Mais oui*, definitely, but she's already disturbed," Victor says with a smirk.

As soon as the three of us cross the threshold to Andre's house, there she is—*grand-mère*—looking like a peasant who's stepped out of a 19th-century French painting. Eyeing me, she asks, "*Qui est–il?*"

"Nana, this is Mark," Andre answers in English. "He's a new friend from the States. I said he could stay here for a night or two."

"Les États?"

"Brooklyn," I say.

"Brookleen?"

"Part of New York City."

"*Le mal. Tu comprends?*" she says, while glowering at me."

"*Oui, Grand-mere*, no trouble."

She shuffles upstairs while we go down to the basement.

"Thanks. I can't believe you all speak French and English."

"Here, most people do. *Grand-mère's Québécoise* to the bone. If it were up to her, she'd never speak a word of English."

Relaxing, we share a Molson or two. Victor puts on *A Love Supreme*, John Coltrane's riveting and soulful album. Coltrane and his quartet are musically expressing their gratitude to and love of God. Coltrane prays in jazz, the way Bach prays in Baroque.

When the record finishes, the three of us sit in silent contemplation.

"Wow," says Victor.

"Once, I saw him play in a club. Usually there's some chattering in the audience, but with Coltrane, it was like being at a symphony concert. Totally quiet, respectful."

"We'd love to visit the city," says Andre.

"You're always welcome at my place."

As Andre gets up to change the record, he says, "Mark, can I ask you something personal?"

"Sure. We're friends."

"Are you Jewish?"

"A hundred percent. Why?"

"I know it's going to sound strange, but I've never hung out with a Jewish person before. Most everyone we grew up with is Catholic. There are Jews in Montreal, but not in Mont Royal."

"Brooklyn's pretty much the same way. The neighborhood I'm from was basically Jewish and Catholic, but the Catholic kids went to parochial school."

"My dad says, 'It's a big world, room enough for everyone,'" Victor says.

"Right on," I say. "It's funny, but you know how sometimes memories come from out of nowhere and just pop into your head? Well, I just flashed on something I haven't thought about in years and years. It's about something that happened to me when I was a kid."

"What?"

"It's like a flashback. Weird, right?"

"I've had those," says Victor.

"OK, here goes. I'm 9." My throat tightens. I stop and start again. "I'm 9, and me and a couple of my pals are playing in this alleyway, which is a shortcut to Caton Avenue. Out of nowhere, these big kids come through and stop. We don't know them at all. The biggest one, a teenager, asks us if we're Jews. Yeah, we say, thinking nothing of it. He nods to his crew and without a moment's hesitation, they start punching and kicking us and calling us 'fuckin' Christ killers.' The big guy hits my friend Bernard so hard he falls on me and my head hits the ground. Our friend, Mitchell, is getting kicked and he starts wailing. Then some lady opens her window and shouts down, 'Cut it out' and the bullies run off as fast as they came. Felt like a nightmare, except we had the bruises to prove it."

."Get hurt bad?"

"We all got banged up pretty good, but we promised to keep it secret and made up some cockamamie story to tell our parents. I was scared shitless for days. Couldn't eat without getting nauseous. If I was outside alone. . . . But over time, it faded away. Andre, when you asked me if I was Jewish, it all came back."

Both of them nod. Andre says, "I'm sorry."

"Here's what I could never get: How could us little kids be Christ killers? He died like 2,000 years before we were born, right? What could we possibly have had to do with that?"

Looking down and then at me, Andre says, "That's what we were taught. From the popes to the priests—the Jews set up Jesus to be crucified, so, all Jews, those then, those now, are guilty for His death."

"But dig this," Victor says, "a couple of years ago, the Vatican changed its mind and said, 'Well, maybe, not really.' "

"Not really? How could it possibly ever have been really?" I say.

"We got hit because we were Catholic."

"Who beat you up? Lutherans? Methodists?"

"No, the nuns, the teachers, the priests."

"One time," Victor goes, "I got hit in front of the whole class because I fell asleep. But I was sick. I had a temperature."

"Mostly they hit the boys. Boys like us."

"Didn't you tell your folks?"

"You'd get double-punished if you did."

"That's insane. Last year, I read some of the New Testament to find out for myself about Jesus. I was amazed by some of the cool things he said and did. He even tried to make the temple get back to basics and stop being a business joint."

Andre goes upstairs and returns with his personal copy of the New Testament. The text is printed in red and black.

"Everything that Jesus said is in red," Andre notes. "I want to read you a couple of my favorite parts, so you can understand why I'm still a Catholic."

He reads aloud from the Sermon on the Mount and several passages from the Gospel of Matthew. When he gets to "It's easier for a camel to go through the eye of a needle than for a rich man to enter heaven," his friend whistles.

"You want to see something?" Victor asks.

"What?"

"*Vient avec moi.*"

July 1969

CROSSES

We go a couple of blocks and then swing into a park overlooking the city.

"What a supercool view," I say.

"*Montréal magnifique*," Andre says. "Victor, St. Joseph's is closed."

"I know."

Turning a corner, a gigantic floodlit church looms before us. It reminds me of St. Patrick's Cathedral in Rockefeller Center.

"You go here? This is your church?"

"St. Joseph's is a basilica," says Andre. "Basilicas are more important than churches. The cardinals could install a pope here instead of at the Vatican."

"When you think of all the time and money they spent on this . . ." Victor starts saying.

"I understand it. They wanted to show God how much they love Him," says Andre.

"What matters is how you act, not what you build," Victor goes. "Anyway, I didn't bring you here to talk about St. Joe's. Follow me."

Near the church, down a quiet lane, sits a small, elegant stone house.

"Who lives here?"

"The priests. The nuns live at the convent."

We stroll past and, then, looking back, Victor whispers, "See that car?"

"The black Mercedes?" Andre replies.

"*Oui*, the brand new, Mercedes 220. You know whose it is?"

"Uh-uh."

"Father Jeremiah's."

"Father Jeremiah has a Mercedes?"

Nodding, Victor says, "Jesus said, 'You can't serve God and money.' So tell me, who's our good Father serving?"

Walking back to the house, they're fuming.

Andre goes, "What about the vow of poverty? What a hypocrite. He should wear a dollar sign instead of a crucifix."

"That's it." Victor says, "We should paint a dollar sign on his car."

We're all too tired to continue this conversation. Victor heads home. Andre and I go upstairs to his room. I climb into the top bunk and fall asleep as soon as my head hits the pillow.

The next day, I go off by myself. First I walk around Mont Royal Park, at the top of which is St. Joseph's Basilica. I wander the trails and observe kids having fun in a playground. This park's like Prospect Park, only cleaner. Following the hill down to street level, I end up at the Montreal Museum of the Arts, where I'm floored by an exhibition of indigenous canoes, all beautifully painted.

Sunday evening, reconvening in his basement, Andre says, "I'm still pissed. Father Jeremiah's a phony. How am I going to stay a good Catholic if our spiritual leaders are full of crap? One day, eating meat on Friday is a mortal sin, which is the worst kind of sin. Then, the Vatican changed its mind and decided, really it's no big deal. Eat what you want."

"Just like that?" I ask.

"It's more complicated, but basically that's what happened. We have to save the church from the hypocrites, like Jesus tried to do."

Taking a piece of paper out of his shirt, Victor shows us a couple of sketches he'd worked on.

Andre points to one that has a cross rising from dollar sign. "That's it. Perfect. It says it all."

From his backpack, Victor takes out a can of red spray paint. "Are you ready to do this?"

"I'm in," says Andre.

"It's your thing," I say. "But if it's going down, I'll cover your backs."

Keeping a distance from one another so as not to arouse notice, Andre goes first, then Victor, then me. When we get to the lane where Father Jeremiah lives, Andre and I stand lookout at either end. Victor steals up to the gleaming Mercedes, spraying the cross and dollar sign on all four doors, the hood and the trunk. Passing St. Joseph's, he makes the cross and dollar sign on its huge wooden doors. Walking at a jog, we return to Andre's. It takes a while for my heart to stop pounding.

At breakfast, Andre retrieves the newspaper from the front door and walks back into the kitchen riveted to a story. He looks shaken. "Oh, my God, last night, in the city, the FLQ, the French Separatists, set off a bomb in a government building." Now reading in a whisper, "In Mont Royal, the doors of St. Joseph's Oratory and a car owned by the diocese were defaced with graffiti. The police are investigating whether these incidents are related."

The blood drains from his face just as *grand-mere* comes into the kitchen. "*Quel es ton problème?*"

"*J'ai un mauvais mal de tête,*" he answers, pointing to his head.

"*Le mal. Une nuit,*" she says, glaring at me. "*Maintenant, il est à deux. Écoutes-moi, il ne sera pas trois.*"

With the newspaper folded under his arm, Andre signals me to follow him down to the basement. "She's not too happy with you staying here."

"I kind of got that."

That evening, Victor joins us to watch the news. A reporter states that the police are no longer connecting the FLQ bombing with our graffiti attack, but he gives no explanation, nor are there any pictures of our handiwork.

"Aren't they going to show the car?" asks Andre.

"What and give people ideas?" Victor says. "Father Jeremiah knows and he knows we know."

"Now's a good time to get lost," I say. "Is there a good place where we can go camping?"

"I know just the spot," Victor replies.

July 1969

FLIGHT PATHS

"Let me show you where it is," says Victor. "Andre, can you go with us?"

"*Mais oui*," Andre replies, "I just have to let my parents know." Making the call, he says "*Je promets*" four or five times before smiling and giving us the thumbs up.

Unfolding a map, Victor circles our destination, a thin blue line leading into a small blue circle, 80 miles north of Montreal. "It's perfect, right by a stream, away from everyone."

Since we're hitching, it takes quite a while to find rides that will accommodate the three of us and our gear. Our longest is from a logging-rig driver, Pierre-Louis, who has a long white beard and red, plaid overalls. Speaking with a heavy French-Canadian accent, he entertains us with lumberjack stories about haunted logging camps and wild women. As he lets us off, Pierre-Louis says, "Life's a big feast, boys. Taste it all."

Near our destination, a passing driver, obviously none too thrilled to be seeing freaks up this way, gives us the finger. The three of us move onto the road and, standing shoulder to shoulder, raise our right fists high—solidarity forever.

Andre says, "I kind of feel like I've had enough of being a revolutionary for a while."

Victor directs us to a general store where we stock up on what we'll need for a couple of days. He leads us to a footpath that runs streamside into the woods. When the path peters out, we follow the water for a mile. At a bend in the channel, Victor stops, looks around, spreads his arms, drops his backpack, and announces, "We're home."

Under a stand of pine trees, upon a deep, soft, fragrant bed of needles, we set up camp. Opting to sleep under the stars, we spread our tarps and sleeping bags on the forest floor. Taking out a foldable shovel, Andre digs a fire pit. Victor and I gather wood.

The water beckons us, so we strip and jump in. Here it's shallow, cool and soothing; around the bend an eddy signals deeper water.

"Is this public land?" I ask. "Didn't see any No Trespassing signs."

"Canadians don't believe in 'em. As long as we carry in, carry out, bury the fire pit—show respect—we're fine."

Andre says, "Our national parks are fantastic, but everyone who camps knows a secret spot like this."

"In the States, there definitely would be No Trespassing signs."

Dinner is hot dogs, baked beans, potato chips, French crullers, and hot chocolate with beer chasers—camp-perfect cuisine.

Andre says, "I was so scared we'd be caught."

"Me, too," I say.

Victor nods. "I got so disgusted that they took the money my parents, your parents and everyone else gave them and went out and bought Father Jeremiah a Mercedes and then they have the nerve to preach to us about being humble and following Jesus."

"I just have to say this," Andre says. "What we did was wrong. Just wrong. It did nothing to change anything. Worse, we could've gotten into big trouble and humiliated our families."

"Let's make an oath that we won't be hypocrites," his pal suggests.

"The non-hypocritic oath," I say.

Clinking our beer bottles, Victor intones and we repeat, "*Pour une vie de fraternité et de la vérité.*"

Settling down, they take out a magnetic chess set and play by firelight.

I hear honking and look up to see six Canada geese, backlit by the moon, flying over us in a V: They're all working together, pulling their weight, knowing exactly where they fit in.

Wouldn't it be great to be one of them? So simple and easy, no conflict, no confusion, just be—that's all, be and survive. Nah, it wouldn't work. I'd be arguing with the leader, picking a different direction, following my own flight path.

I close my eyes, and "follow your flight path" reverberates in my dreams.

In the morning, I find myself wondering if my presence wasn't a trigger, a catalyst, for our commando raid. Might they have been trying to impress me? I hope not. I guess it's best for me to get back to my life and leave *mes amies* to theirs.

The following day, as we make our way back, I tell them, "OK you two. You men are in charge of keeping Montreal righteous. I gotta go. Someone's got to keep an eye on Brooklyn."

On the Greyhound, I realize I never gave them my phone number, nor did they ask. *C'est la vie.*

July 1969

"Slow down. You're gonna get us killed," I shout, as Ezra, my psychedelic artist friend, speeds his Saab convertible down the serpentine Ohayo Mountain Road.

"Celeste, the astrologer, said I'm going to live to be 100," he shouts back.

"Yeah, well, she told me, 'Beware of crazy drivers.'"

Around another hairpin turn, a ramshackle house with a red barn comes into view. Ezra jolts the car to a stop.

"Bingo."

In stark contrast to the panic-inducing ride, things are serene here. People are sitting outside listening to two long-hairs play their guitars; a small child, naked, is chasing another; several women, wearing long, colorful skirts, are standing and talking.

Ezra says, "Told you this commune is one hip scene."

Entering the house, we encounter a man who's trying to look a lot like Jesus. Ezra introduces me. "This is Clark, he and his lady Ava started the Ohayo Mountain Family and keep it grooving. Clark's a painter, too."

Shaking my hand, Clark goes, "Peace, bro, any friend of Ezra's is like well, like, y'know."

"Likewise."

The two of them go off to see Clark's latest paintings. I wander outside and listen to the guys with the guitars sing Irish folk songs. Off in the distance sit other Catskill Mountains dressed in greens and browns. I lie on my back and try to identify each tree that surrounds me by its leaves.

Next thing I know I'm waking up, Ezra car's gone, and my backpack and sleeping bag are leaning against a tree. Maybe they went somewhere. Maybe Ezra had to leave. *That's the way it be's sometimes.* No big deal, I'll camp outside, find a bed inside or hitch back to my friend's house.

Since I always like exploring new places, I take a look around. The dining room has wall-sized abstract paintings, signed by Clark, featuring colorful, irregular shapes intersecting each other, like stoned Venn diagrams. Where Ezra's work is delicate and unique, Clark's seems haphazard and imitative.

In the dining room, instead of a table and chairs, there are cushions stacked against the walls and a long narrow table with silverware in glass jars, stacks of mismatched dishes, plastic glasses, and napkin holders. Above the doorway to the kitchen is a woodcarving that reads "O.M. sweet OM."

The kitchen's bustling with activity as four women are deep into cooking a meal. Beyond the kitchen, two small rooms have been turned into living quarters. Upstairs are three or four more bedrooms. In the backyard, there are a couple of cars, a motorcycle, three bikes, tents of varying sizes, clotheslines, and two psychedelically decorated outhouses.

The Ohayo Mountain Family is a commune, the kind of place where everyone is supposed to live and work together for the common good. Private property is kept at a minimum, possessions are shared, and egos are left at the door. The idea is that the whole is greater than the sum of its parts. But at this commune I wonder, what is the whole and what is the goal?

Continuing my circle, I wander into the barn where windows have been cut along its sides. Multicolored bedspreads, flags, and batikked and tie-dyed sheets transform the hay loft and animal stalls into small personalized sleeping spaces. I guess everyone needs a place to call their own. While this little homestead is clearly being used to its max, things feel vibrant, orderly, together.

Back at the house, I bump into Clark. "Ezra had to split. You're welcome to join us for dinner."

Following him into the dining room, the members of the commune, most of whom seem to be in their late teens and early twenties, are sitting on the pillows. Helping myself to a plate of spaghetti, tomato sauce, vegetables, homemade bread, and salad, I sit against a wall. People wait to begin eating.

Tapping a small gong, a dark-haired, smiling-faced beauty says, "Hi. I'm Ava. I see a couple of new faces. The Ohayo Mountain Family, the O.M. for short, welcomes you."

Clark adds, "May your step be soft and joyful and your footprint small."

After dinner, a donation basket is passed around and after tossing in three bucks, I go into the kitchen and offer to help with the pots and pans. A very cute, black chick with the world's softest-looking Afro smiles at me. "A man who actually does kitchen work."

"My mom always said, 'Housework's work, needs to get done, don't matter who does it.'"

"Right on."

The noise and activity level go down with the sun. Some people read, others write, some sit in small groups doing Tarot readings or tossing *I Ching* coins. It's like a very mellow library.

I remind myself I need to figure out where I'm sleeping. I spot the two guitarists.

"Hey, man," I say.

"Hey, bro."

"You cats sounded good. I'm Mark."

"Cool. Call me River."

"I'm Dennis," says the other who speaks with a brogue, "Can't go wrong with good Irish ballads."

"I dig it. I'm a Clancy Brothers fan, myself," I say. "I kind of got dropped off here, need a place to crash."

River nods toward the chick I met in the kitchen. "Talk to Carmen."

Figuring she's in charge of sleeping arrangements, I say, "River said you're the one to ask about finding a place to sleep."

Looking me up and down, she goes, "Maybe . . . but first tell me about you."

"I'm Mark from Brooklyn."

"Carmen from Oakland."

"Nice to make your acquaintance."

"Likewise."

"Been coming to Woodstock for a while . . ." Carmen's blank expression tells me I'm heading nowhere fast, so I switch gears. "Well, this September I'm going to be a brand new, New York City second-grade teacher."

"No way."

"For sure."

"Really?" she asks.

"Board of Ed certified."

"With that long hair?"

"So far."

"Cool."

"Cool?"

"Cool, but don't get no ideas," she says.

Leading me to the barn, she takes me to a bed that has an African print wall hanging as a divider. "You can stay here with me."

Peeking around the corner, she says to the couple on the other side of the divider, "This is Mark, he's sharing my bed tonight and nothing else."

"Nothing else," I repeat.

By morning, the two of us are cuddled up together like two contented kittens.

August 1969

TOV

With his curly red hair and beard, twinkling blue eyes, bulging belly, beige robe, green sash, bracelets on one wrist and a bandana on the other, Tov looks like one of Robin Hood's Merry Band. But his lisp, which comes and goes, his longing looks at River, the guitarist, and his friendly, non-flirtatious way with the women suggest he's a member of a different group of merry men.

I like him. He's very funny and laughs at my jokes. More than that, he's the only other cat who scrubs the pots and pans. While the other guys talk about how they support the Women's Movement, none cook or clean up.

Walking outside after a stint in the kitchen, I complain to him. "For the counterculture thing to work, we all have to walk the walk. Either men and women are equal or they're not. Either we're in this together or we're not. What I see here is men do men's work, women do women's work and a lot of people just hang out and do nothing. Right, Tov?"

He shrugs. "That's not my real name."

"I know in Hebrew, *tov* means good. I figured you were raised Orthodox."

"My real name's Mitchell," he says, extending his hand, as if we're meeting for the first time. "Mitchell Israel Abrams from Midwood, pleased to meet you."

"I'm from the borough too. Y'know, I've had this feeling I know you from somewhere."

We play Brooklyn Geography—I went to Erasmus Hall High School, he to Midwood High.

I ask, "What junior high?"

"Ditmas?"

"That's it, me too."

Turns out he was a year behind me.

"Maybe you'll know the answer to this. It's bugged me for years." I say. "Ditmas Junior High isn't on Ditmas Avenue. They built it a block away on Courtelyou Road. So, why did they name it Ditmas?"

"Once, I *courtel-you*," he says, "but not anymore." Getting serious, he adds, "At Ditmas, I called myself Mickey."

"Mickey?" Then peering through his beard to his face, I go, "Oh, my God, I remember you. You used to hang around with Samantha DiCarlo and Sam Lazarus." I remember the boy who wore makeup and pretended it was to hide his pimples and the girl who wore her hair super-short. "He called himself Sonny and she called herself Sam, right?"

"Go figure. Sam hated his name and she loved it."

Now extending my hand, I say, "Howdy, pardner."

Tov says, "My father kicked me out on the spot when he found me in bed with another boy. Remember Artie Spivack? It was him."

"Artie? My handball partner Artie? Him?"

He nods. "Only 16, been on my own since then. My father screamed, 'Never come back. You're dead to us. Praise be to God for our two daughters.'"

"Unbelievable. Mine didn't kick me out, but living at home was totally lame. Like living in the Tower of Babel—we spoke the same words, but they meant totally different things. Hey, but look, we're both here and we're both hard workers."

"Hard work, easy work, what choice did I have? It was dreadful. You can't imagine how alone I felt, how ashamed, how . . ." and with that, he pushes up the bandana covering his left wrist revealing a horizontal scar. "A friend, another homo Jew, but ritzier, from Westchester, found me in the bathroom, I was so drunk . . . bandaged me up, took me to his place, fed me chicken soup, sobered me up, and got me to his psychiatrist. Would you believe, a homosexual psychiatrist?"

"Why not?"

"I was like, y'know, born again, but it wasn't by our God or Jesus, it was by other queers. It took a lot of love and time for me to see that being different doesn't mean being bad. I mean isn't that what they taught us? Jews are God's chosen people, we're different."

"Jews, gentiles, from where I sit, they're all full of shit. They say: follow the commandments, but then they only follow the ones they like. It's all about power and control, part of the power structure."

"No longer Mitchell or Mickey, I needed a new name. Well, I'd never intentionally harm anyone, I mean, I won't even eat meat, I'm good. So I became Tov."

"Tov it is. How'd you get here?"

"The guy I'm was with works at the framing shop. I got all jealous, we got into this big fight. Ava's my yoga teacher and when she saw how upset I was she said I could come stay here. Y'know, Mark, the other guys may not work in the kitchen, but they've been totally cool with me."

"That counts."

"Big time."

August 1969

POWWOW

Clark works hard at seeming mystical. To further his allure, he wears a robe and sandals, stays aloof from the daily goings-on and speaks infrequently. Ava, his wife and co-leader, is his opposite. She's organized, approachable, and always involved in everything.

When Clark deigns to speak I expect to hear cosmic pronouncements, but invariably what's on his mind is something like, "We're really low on raisins."

So at dinner tonight, when I see him dressed in jeans, a denim shirt, and a tie-dyed bandana on his head, I sense something's up.

After Ava leads us in grace, Clark speaks, "We're calling a powwow tonight at the fire pit. It's important. Head down there after dinner."

"Please, don't ask us about it now," Ava says. "We want to tell everyone at the same time."

Carmen and I head to the fire pit with another couple, River and Lanie. It's my first group meeting, so I ask what they're like.

"Clark and Ava only call them when they have to," Lanie says. "But once it gets rolling, it's like a Quaker meeting. People can bring up pretty much anything."

Arms around each other, River and Lanie match strides as they stroll down the path. After dropping out of Penn State together, they came here seeking a new kind of life.

Carmen and I are like halfway a couple. Whenever I try to find out more about her past, her fantastic smile evaporates and she admonishes me. "All we have is now, let's not waste it by talking about what was." That doesn't work for me.

Everyone is sitting in a circle. Ava starts chanting, "*Om-shanti-shanti-om*" and we all join in. Joints are passed around and the vibes get soft and easy.

Holding a Buddha statuette, she says, "Buddha is here to help us stay centered and to remind us that being open works best. Whoever's holding Buddha gets to speak. We like to pass it from woman to man and back, keeps us united."

Clark adds, "Couple of crew chiefs got stuff to discuss. Ava and me are up last."

Manny, the head of the fixer-upper crew, stands. He wears his hair in a short Afro and sports a Fu Manchu moustache. I've worked with him on a number of projects and respect his know-how and work ethic. Hailing from the Bronx, Manny's earned his muscular arms and oversized hands working in the building trades. He's been at the O.M. since the spring.

"The pink outhouse is sinking," he says. "Sinking fast. Better hope you're not the one who takes *that* elevator ride to the basement." People laugh, but not Manny. "Tomorrow morning, we gotta dig a new ditch, fill in the old ditch, and move that dayglow sucker to its new home. I need a crew of six."

Several people shout out their names to indicate they're in, then quiet returns. Manny's determined. "I ain't had much *edjemacation*, but I can count past four. Four don't do it. Need some more." A couple of others volunteer. "*Mañana*, after breakfast."

He hands Buddha to this new girl who asks, "What's that big gigantic lake at the bottom of the hill?"

"It's the Ashokan Reservoir," someone says. "Fifty years ago, New York City bought the land, forced the people out, and drowned their towns to make it. Ever wonder where Manhattan gets its water? Wonder no more."

Taking the Buddha, Susan, the head gardener, says, "We gotta weed the vegetable garden."

"Weeds are just plants you don't like," some chick calls out.

"If you know how to make spaghetti sauce from dandelions, tell us, because we make it from tomatoes, our tomatoes," Susan goes.

Rising, Lanie says, "Weeds are cool. They can grow everywhere else, just not in our vegetable patch."

People shout out their names. Susan sits down satisfied.

As the dark descends, Clark rises. "We've been through a lot, but we've kept our spirit strong."

"There a problem?" Dennis asks.

Ava gets up. "Clark's always so dramatic. It's nothing bad. This morning, Wavy Gravy, the leader of the Hog Farm commune, called us. They're with the Merry Pranksters at the Woodstock festival site and they need our help."

A murmur ripples through the group.

Someone calls out, "Ken Kesey with them?"

"Wavy didn't say," responds Clark.

Ken Kesey and the Merry Pranksters are our high priests of hijinks. The Pranksters established their rep as a street theater group mocking America's pro-war, anti-love culture. Kesey became famous with his book *One Flew over the Cuckoo's Nest*. When the Pranksters and Kesey connected in San Francisco, it was a trip. Followed by another trip and another, until they got this far-out idea to paint a school bus in psychedelic colors and take an actual trip—a west to east, cross-country pilgrimage. Their mission was to urge America's youth to embrace lives filled with spontaneity and cooperation and reject lives of conformity and alienation. For them, LSD hits the spot. With music festivals and alternate life styles popping up all over the place, the seeds they planted seem to have taken root.

"They're in Woodstock?" Tov asks.

"No, not Woodstock Woodstock. Woodstock the music festival. Y'know," and here Clark uses his fingers for quotation marks, "Three Days of Peace and Music."

Everyone starts talking at once. Holding the Buddha high, Ava waits for the chatter to subside. "It was supposed to be nearby in Saugerties, but the landowner chickened out. Then Wallkill agreed to hold the festival, but the locals went bat-shit crazy and killed the permit."

Clark picks up the thread, "And at the very last possible moment, baby, just as that ship of righteous joy was about to plunge down that abyss . . . boom! White Lake said 'Yes.' It's a-happenin', people."

"I've been following this," River stands, raising his voice to be heard, "A friend of mine has a ticket outlet in the city and he told me tickets are flying out the door. A hundred thousand people might show up, maybe twice that."

Dennis says, "They've booked the Who, the Dead, Jefferson Airplane, Janis, Creedence Clearwater, the Band and get this, Jimi. Name a band, good chance they'll be there. It's going to be a total blast."

Again, the chatter starts up.

Ava waits. "Wavy Gravy said they're working, like crazy, setting up camping areas and food kitchens in the cow pastures. It starts on Friday, only just five days away. They need us."

River shouts, "The biggest fuckin' rock festival ever. Ever."

"A gathering of the tribes," someone adds.

Putting his arm over Ava's shoulder, Clark brings it home, "So, if you want to work your ass off all day and boogie all night, be on our school bus at 7 a.m. sharp, 'cause at 7:01, we'll be trucking on down that highway."

August 1969

Woodstock

ROCK IT

Monday, August 11, 1969, 7 a.m.

Our old yellow school bus is idling in front of the farm-house. Clark, our leader, is behind the wheel. Seated directly behind him is his wife, Ava. Manny, the work crew boss, is studying a map.

Climbing aboard, I look at Manny, "Now hold it a second. Didn't you say we had to move the pink outhouse today?"

"Yeah, I know. Move the stinky outhouse or go to a dynamite music festival. Tough choice. I tossed and turned for almost a second on that one. Listen, that shitter ain't going nowhere, but making this Woodstock thing happen, man, chance of a lifetime."

Ava says, "Seven on the dot."

Manny calls out, "And away we go."

"Let's rock it," Clark says, tooting the horn to announce our departure.

Yesterday, the Hog Farm commune, out of New Mexico, invited us to help them set up the Woodstock Music Festival and we're on our way.

Twenty members of the Ohayo Mountain Family are on board, chattering like a jungle of jitterbugs. Not everyone decided to come. Like Tov. Last night, he confided to me that he accidently on purpose bumped into the guy he was involved with and they're meeting for a drink tonight. And like my almost girlfriend, Carmen.

"I don't like crowds," she said and that was that. So this morning, after giving her my Brooklyn phone number, we hugged and said a tearless goodbye.

Clark is driving so slowly that we get passed by every car and truck on the road. When a farm tractor starts gaining on us, River calls, "Clark, didn't you say, 'Let's rock it'?"

"This bus is a cop magnet," Clark responds. "I'm five miles below the speed limit and that's where I'm staying. Ain't giving the Man no excuse to stop us."

"Stay cool, people," Ava says. "We're on the Yellow Brick Road."

So, after a painfully slow, consistently bumpy, but scenically beautiful, two-hour bus ride through the Catskill Mountains, we roll down a country road until we come upon a construction site, adjacent to a very large, sloping pasture, teeming with activity.

"This must be the place," Clark goes, pulling up to a mobile home/construction office with a sign on its door that says "Woodstock."

Alighting from the bus, he says, "I'll be back in a minute."

OFF THE BUS

Monday, August 11, 1969, noon

Clark climbs back on board along with this tall, solidly built cat wearing a tool belt, a braided ponytail to his waist, and a big smile on his dark, sunburnt face.

"*Hola, compadres.* I'm Grayhawk. Glad you're here. Need all the braves and squaws we can get. Festival's just four days away."

Directing our bus through the pasture, up a hill, and around a stand of trees, Grayhawk leads us to a field dotted with painted buses, campers, and cars. We grab our stuff and follow him to a camping area filled with tipis, army tents, pup tents and lean-tos. Work crews are busy on an assortment of projects.

"Welcome home," Grayhawk says.

Jogging over to us is this older cat—thin, weathered, mid-30s, wearing a well-worn, straw cowboy hat. "You must be the Ohayo Mountain Family? I'm Wavy Gravy with the Hog Farm. Hope Grayhawk told you it's gonna take a miracle to get everything ready in time." Then, with a warm, confident, toothless smile, he adds, "But, hot dog, if we all ain't miracle workers."

"We're here to help," Ava says.

"If you know how to swing a hammer," Wavy says, "Go see Rob, the guy with the red bandana. Cooks, go see Kasha." He points to a buxom chick in a green, sleeveless T-shirt. "Not sure? No problem. Stay with me. We got tons to do."

"Where do we sleep?" I ask.

"Army tents. Pick one that's got room and move in."

Carrying my gear, I peek inside a couple—full and full. A ways away from the central hub, there's a khaki tent that's half-way full, so I stake my spot by unrolling my sleeping bag and dropping my backpack next to it. Outside, I spend a couple of minutes noting the nearby tents and some other landmarks, so that I'll be able to find my way back here. The sun's shining and I'm not high, but neither of these conditions is likely to hold for long.

Lanie and Ava go to help Kasha organize a food tent that's covered in clear plastic. River and I lend a hand unloading two step vans filled to the roof with 50-pound bags of brown rice, oatmeal and sugar, sacks of potatoes, bushels of vegetables, packages and packages of bread, industrial-size jars of peanut butter and jelly, restaurant service boxes of tea and instant coffee, barrels of soy sauce, cases of salt, gallons of cooking oil. As soon we unload the vans, a dairy truck pulls up, stocked with milk bottles stacked in wooden crates, pound blocks of butter, large wedges of cheese, and dozens and dozens of eggs. These are from Max Yasgur, the farmer whose land we're on.

One large dome-shaped food kitchen, equipped with propane burners, is already in place. This is where the cooking will take place. Manny and a crew are assembling food service kiosks where people will line up for meals. Each has work spaces, storage places, and serving counters. Serving bowls and kitchen utensils wait to be put in place. Power lines strung on poles provide electricity for refrigeration, lights, and tools. Aside from a joke now and then, a break for water, a toke on a joint, everyone stays focused and works the whole day through.

Today's Monday, Friday is show time. We'd best be ready.

Tuesday, August 12, 1969, dawn

At the break of dawn, I'm awakened to the sound of a fog horn. Fog horn? I'm in a pasture in upstate New York, a good 100 miles from the ocean. No matter, it's time to get up. I wander down to the hub where people are in a semicircle facing this couple. They both have braided, dirty blond hair, the guy is sporting a short beard. *Ah, Californians.*

"Hi, I'm Tom Law. This is my wife, Lisa. We're with the Hog Farm. Every day will start like this—doing yoga, inhaling and exhaling together. It's for ourselves and for the festival."

Lisa Law picks it up, "Now's the time to start sowing seeds of peace. We gotta spread 'em every day to create a strong, loving aura for the festival. Let's face old Mr. Sun and do our Sun Salutation. We salute him like this." She and Tom stretch their arms above their heads.

What the hell. I put out my cigarette and, clumsily, join in. I've tried yoga any number of times. I know it works. Only, I can never get myself to practice it on any kind of a regular basis.

When the session is over, Wavy Gravy stands up holding a bullhorn. Along with his straw cowboy hat, he's wearing a white jumpsuit with a red star on the back.

"Sorry to be using this," he says, pointing to the loud speaker, "but my voice wants to go back to New Mexico. Hey, but, dig this. Michael Lang and Artie Kornfield, the guys running this show, came to us because they were freaked out. Sure, they had the money and the music lined up, but then it hit them like a pie in the face—how were they going to take care of all the thousands and thousands of kids who were coming? They heard about what we did at the Trips Festival and they knew if anyone knew, we knew, so they just about begged us to help."

"That's the truth. I was there," Tom Law says.

"We had three conditions—One, no cops inside the site, we take care of our own. Two, people gonna get hungry, so write us a check and we'll go to New York City and stock up on food and equipment and three, don't pay us. This'll only work if we do it for love."

Grayhawk shouts, "Y'all down with this?"

We respond with cheers and applause.

Wavy continues, "More freaks'll be here than anyone ever dreamed existed. Don't matter how hard the shit comes crashing down, and, believe me, it will. We gotta make it land soft. Instead of the police force, we gonna *be* the Please Force."

Lisa Law goes last. "Paramahansa Yogananda said, 'Work is the physical manifestation of love,' and we definitely need a ton of fuckin' manifesting going on here to get this place ready for the party. May all the higher powers bless us and may we be worthy of their faith. Now let's get to work."

DAN THE MAN

Tuesday, August 12, 1969, late morning

On line for breakfast, Manny asks me if I can work with his crew today. I say sure. Sitting down with a half-dozen guys, including several from Ohayo Mountain and some other cats I don't yet know, the conversation is about today's assignment.

I overhear Dennis, from my commune, saying, ". . . and since I did some surveying work back in Ireland, they asked me to lay out the best path up the hill to the new camping areas."

"We got to make it so an ambulance can get over the hill," Manny says. "Dennis'll mark it and then we'll clear the brush, big rocks, take down any small trees, and smooth it out."

"Sounds pretty primitive," River says. "We digging any ditches for runoff?"

"Need a back hoe for that," a heavyset freak says. "Manny, if you get one, I can run it."

"I'll ask. Mark and me will bop down to the office to pick up tools."

"Let's start clearing away those stones," Dennis says.

Going toward the stage area, I'm amazed to see how many more people have arrived. Some trek up the hill to the camping areas while others fan out to the pasture that faces the stage. Passing each other, the smiles and nods come naturally. Fellow freaks. Family.

There's a bevy of activity as food vendors, souvenir stands, and lefty revolutionaries build booths to push their wares—hot dogs, T-shirts, and diatribes.

Outside the construction office is this guy with a dark beard and a rapidly receding hairline who looks like a beat poet from the '50s.

Manny tells me, "He's basically in charge of all the construction."

Finishing up with two or three others before turning to us, Manny says, "How's Dan the Man today?"

"More we do, more we have to do. What's up?"

"We're building that wide path up the hill to the new camping areas. Need some tools. Oh, and if you got a backhoe, we got an operator who can dig a trench for runoff."

Dan shakes his head. "Extra backhoe, you're a laugh a minute." Taking us around back to a locked, fenced-in tool storage area, he motions toward the shovels, pickaxes, and bow saws. "Take what you need, but you gotta return them. Gotta. They're more valuable than gold."

As we load the wheelbarrows with the tools, Dan goes, "We all gotta be thinking: Can I do this faster? 'Cause the one thing we can't buy is time." Pointing at a van, he asks, "Either of you drive stick?"

We both say yeah, no hassle.

"Take it and drive the tools up the hill."

Manny says, "Mark, you drive it. That way, after we unload, you can return it."

With people walking ahead of us, driving uphill takes patience. I keep my right foot on the gas and my left tap dances between the clutch and the brake, finally we bouncy-bounce our way to the crew.

Dropping off the tools, I ask River to go ahead and shoo away people as I drive back to the office.

"Great. That was fast," says Dan. "Hog Farmers rock."

No point in telling him we're with the Ohayo Mountain Family.

As we walk away, he calls us back. "I'm losing my mind. What else is new? Anyway, first thing tomorrow morning, I need you to take the van and go into Monticello and buy up as much bottled water as you can. The electricians and carpenters need it. There'll be boxes of stuff for us at the hardware store too."

"You sure the van will still be here?" I ask.

"It better be."

"Sounds good," River says. "See you in the morning."

River and I trot back to our crew. We're back on the road gang.

Tuesday, August 12, 1969, night

As the sun kisses the day good night, everyone lines up at the plastic sheeted, dome-topped, field kitchen coming away with plates filled with bulgur wheat and veggies. Sitting down with the Ohayo Mountain folks, we share about what we've been doing.

Tara, who at the commune kept to herself, seems to have undergone a transformation. "I'm working with the banging and cussing crew," she says. "The crowds size is gonna be off the wall, so we're putting together more food kitchens."

"I'm worried," Lanie says. "What if we can't do it? Can't get it ready in time?"

"We'll look like fuck-ups, that's what," Ava replies.

"Not look like, we'll be fuck-ups," adds Manny. "Goodbye revolution, hello riots."

"Hey people, let's keep it righteous. Let's keep the faith," goes River.

"He's right," I add. "Just gotta keep on keeping on. No other choice."

Sounds of drumming catch our attention. In the hub's center, there's a bonfire with a circle of women drumming together. This thin chick, with braids sticking straight up like a TV antenna, starts a rhythm and the others pick it up, wind it up, and spin it around until it becomes a polyrhythmic whirlwind, full-tilt and wild. People start dancing, clapping, shouting, and banging on anything they can.

After a while, the pulse ebbs and slows to a stop. In the lull before they start up again, several fully costumed clowns noisily fall out of a nearby tent. They're wrestling with this huge cardboard box that seems to have a mind of its own. The clowns stumble, doing pratfalls, while the box careens toward the fire. Instead of being alarmed, people are laughing and cheering.

I hear murmurs, "The Merry Pranksters."

Flying out of the top of the box come bags and bags of marshmallows. The drummers start up a Latin rhythm and the

Pranksters start tearing the bags apart and squashing the marsh-mallows together into a gigantic, soft, white ball, skewering it with branches whittled from trees. It's about to be roasted when Wavy Gravy intones into the bullhorn, "This is a sacrament. Manna from heaven. Everyone who partakes in it is, now and forever, a member of a new species of homo sapiens: *familia woodstockae*."

Placed over the fire, the marshmallow Eucharist flares up and burns brightly. Using smaller branches, the sticky, charred mass gets divided and passed around. We each take a bite of the singed treat. A perfect freak ritual—silly and serious.

Someone starts singing "Old MacDonald," and we all join in sounding like a class of kindergartners, albeit a huge and very twisted one. Taking the bullhorn, Ava sings, "And on the farm, we had a swami, E-I-E-I-O, with an Om here and an Om there, here an Om, there an Om, everywhere an Om Om . . ."

With stars twinkling, a cool breeze blowing, the sounds of joy wafting through the air, camaraderie thick enough to hug, I feel utterly alive and deeply moved. With all this positive energy, Woodstock just has to work.

It's time to crash. Remembering my landmarks, I make my way back to the tent where sounds of sleeping fill the air. Quietly undressing, I slide into my sleeping bag—bone-tired and content beyond words. Is this the best I've ever felt? Who knows? But, even having such a thought is, well, cosmic.

CAL CONGA GAL

Wednesday, August 13, 1969, morning

Standing in front of me on the breakfast line is the pretty blonde with the antenna pigtails who led last night's drumming circle.

"Great drumming, totally cool," I say.

Turning to look at me, she says, "Thanks. Playing for people is new for us. Mostly, we jam in the backroom of a bookstore."

"One summer, I was a parkee in this Puerto Rican neighborhood in Brooklyn, and, man, those *congueros* would show up with their congas, bongos, claves, whatever, and jam like they were on fire. Just like last night. You lit a flame under everyone's butt."

Meeting my eyes, she goes, "Everyone was lit to begin with."

"*Touché*. . . . Your drums look homemade?"

"Half and half. We get soy sauce barrels from Chinatown, clean and dry them out, then this drum maker we know cuts them down and adds the skins and hardware."

We sit down together.

"How'd you get here?"

"Two weeks ago, one of the Pranksters, maybe it was Rob, I can't remember, came to our drumming circle. He told us about Woodstock and said there was room on their bus for us. It sounded fuckin' far out, so most of us packed up and hopped on and here we are. The bus ride from Haight-Ashbury took forever, like six days."

"Only took us two hours," I say. "But we drove so slow, it felt like a week."

River comes by. "Hey bro, we told Dan the Man we'd help him out."

Tied around River's left wrist is a red cloth adorned with a flying pig. "What's that?" I ask.

"ID, says we're with the Hog Farm. Makes it easier to get stuff."

"Anyone could make one," Cal Conga Gal says.

"Exactly. That's why it's so cool," he replies. "Means something and nothing at the same time."

"I better go," I say. "Nice talking to you."

"Likewise."

On the way to the construction office, my buddy says, "That chick is hot. What's her name?"

"Don't know." I look back at the empty spot where we had just been. "At least not yet."

MONTICELLO

Wednesday, August 13, 1969, noon

Dan the Man is standing exactly where he was yesterday, wearing the same clothes, and I swear, talking with the same people. Only difference, the bags under his eyes have gotten bigger and darker.

"Hey, Dan, you look like shit," says this guy in an official Woodstock T-shirt.

"You ain't lookin' so pretty either," Dan calls back. Then, addressing River and me, he goes, "I haven't slept in two days, how am I supposed to look?"

We remind him he asked us to take the van to Monticello for bottled water and other supplies.

"Thanks for remembering." Going into the mobile office, he emerges with a wad of cash and a sheet of paper. "Buy as much water as you can. Stop at Wyde Lumber, they have some boxes for us. Don't got time to take any chances, so make sure everything on this order form is in the boxes. If you got any money left, buy me a couple of cartons of Marlboros."

Once in the van, River says, "Can it only be two days since we got here? Man, this scene is intense."

"Intense, but good. Know what I dig? Being with other worker bees. Look at all we're getting done."

Driving on the road parallel to the site, River says, "Look at those measly fences. They're practically nothing. No way they'll keep people out."

"Dan and the others must be hip to it, but what can they do? If like a hundred thousand people show up, how they gonna keep them out? Shoot 'em?"

River agrees. "Can you picture thousands of freaks, tickets or no tickets, coming all this way and then just turning around and going home? Ain't gonna happen, man."

Going to a couple of supermarkets, we buy up most of their bottled water. The hardware store has four big boxes for us, and one of the clerks helps us double-check the order. Completing our assignment, we pick up a couple of cartons of cigarettes.

Handing River a pack and taking one myself, I say, "We deserve a tip."

"A tip? Buy low, sell high. That's my dad's favorite joke," River says.

Since I have some money on me, I tell River I'll treat him to lunch at the diner on the main drag. We slide quietly into a booth looking out on the street.

The cashier's saying, "Every one of these kids has been courteous and paid their bill. What else do you want?"

"Would it hurt if they got a haircut? I mean would it?" answers a middle-aged woman.

A man in a seersucker suit says, "They're bringing people here. Economically speaking, it's a blessing."

"Blessing? You call smoking drugs a blessing?"

"From a commercial perspective, that's all I'm saying."

"Where the hell did all these hippies come from anyway?"

"That's easy, outer space."

Our young waitress smiles conspiratorially at us. "It's a riot. Goes on like this all day long. 'It's good.' 'It's the end of the world.' Saturday, after work, my boyfriend and me are going."

We order breakfast for lunch—eggs, home fries, coffee and top it off with chocolate milk shakes.

Looking around, I say, "I know this joint. I ate here like years ago, when I was nine or ten."

"Here?"

"We must have been on our way to or from some hotel. Back then, Monticello was the summer capital for Jews. Everyone went to the Catskill Mountains to get away from the blazing city heat. Where'd your family go?"

"Cape Cod or my mother's family in New Jersey."

"There were all these hotels and bungalow colonies. During the day, us kids swam, played softball, basketball, went on nature walks, or just horsed around, while our folks took a *platz*, sat in lawn chairs, chatted with other guests, maybe played a little gin rummy or pinochle."

"I heard about 'the mountains.' They had these great entertainers, right?"

"All the places had lounges. Comedians, like Alan King, tried out new material, or a small combo set up and the next Vic Damone or Patti Page would sing their hearts out. Once I saw my folks doing a slow fox trot together, dancing real close, being, what can I say, being sexy. Blew my mind. That never happened back in Brooklyn."

"Good food too, huh?" River says.

"I can see the look of satisfaction on my dad's face. He's eating lunch—chilled borscht topped with a dab of sour cream, a corned beef sandwich, German potato salad, then washing it all down with a cold Schaefer beer. For my mom, no shopping, no cooking, no dishes. Heaven. But then, boom, it changed. Everyone started going to Florida, to Miami, or as the older Jews called it 'Mimi Bich.' "

Although it took us less than a half hour to get here, the road back is crowded with vehicles. At a jammed intersection, a state trooper is directing traffic. Honking, I wave River's red bandana with the pig insignia. "Officer, we're Hog Farmers bringing in water and supplies, please let us through." He nods, stops traffic, and waves us on.

Back at the construction office, Dan looks inside the van. "You guys did great. Thanks a million."

Handing him the cigarette cartons, I tell him, "River and me each took a pack."

"Here, take a couple more. You cats are great." Then looking at me, he says, "You're Mark, right? Do me a solid. We may need you for other truck runs, so check in with me from time to time."

Wednesday, August 13, 1969, afternoon

River and I climb the hill to go back to the hub. Since this morning new signposts with arrows are in place pointing to Groovy Way, Gentle Path and, of course, High Way.

"I hope they don't give out tent numbers." River says. "Should we check in with Manny or Tom Law?"

"Truth be told, I'm in no mood to work."

"Me neither."

A steady stream of newcomers, some carrying camping equipment, make their way up Groovy Path. We tag along to see how things are going and enter a small field that's filling up with tents and jury-rigged lean-to's put together with tree branches and pieces of discarded lumber.

A couple of freaks ask us where they can get water, some food, make a phone call, find a Port-O-San. River asks, "How come you're asking us?"

"Easy, you're got a red pig cloth hanging out your back pocket."

Over a ridge, come these two guys and two girls, all wet, wild-eyed, and bare-chested.

"What's happening?" River shouts.

"A pond. Water's cold and great," says one of the guys.

"All together in the altogether," laughs one of the chicks, crossing her arms across her torso.

That's all we need to hear. River and I start trotting. The closer we get, the louder the sounds of splashing and merriment. It's a sea of wet hair, big smiles, and floating breasts.

Lanie is there. "Honey, c'mon in," she purrs to River.

He undresses in a flash and cannonballs into the water. Someone passes a joint around and I take a toke, but instead of going swimming, I lie down. Closing my eyes, I nod off. Drops of water on my face wake me up.

Shielding my eyes from the sun, I see it's Cal Conga Gal using her pigtails as a sprinkler. "You scared to get wet? It feels great. Just jump in."

"Tell me your name and I'm game."

"Candy."

"From Candace?"

"Uh-uh. When I was little, whenever my mom asked me what I wanted for dinner, I said candy. So it became my nickname."

"A girl who knows what she wants."

I strip and dive in. Swimming around, we meet up with Lanie and River. Lanie says to Candy, while winking at me, "Mark's cute, and he's a real good guy."

After a while, we all sense it's time to get back. There's stuff to do, lots and lots of stuff to do.

Candy gets out of the water, turns her back to me and slips into her short shorts and tank top. I shake myself off and pull on my jeans and T-shirt. As we stroll back to the hub, she takes my hand and leads me to her tent. Inside it's cool and empty.

Putting a finger across her lips, she whispers, "Let's take a little time for us."

"You OK? Birth control?"

"I'm on the pill."

And with that we kiss, undress and embrace, completely, enchantingly, ecstatically. That night, I move my sleeping bag and backpack next to hers.

LUCKY

Thursday, August 14, 1969, morning

At breakfast, Candy is enjoying oatmeal stretched out on her stomach, supported by her elbows. She reminds me of a mountain cat—her body is sleek, her eyes take in the landscape, her head turns to catch some distant sound. She's at once relaxed and ready to spring.

I lean down. "I like how we cuddled up together last night."

"Me, too. We need a tent of our own."

"Definitely, but how to find one?"

She shrugs, "Where there's a will . . ."

"There's usually been a funeral."

"C'mon, Brooklyn, keep that freak flag flying. Let's look around."

So we start peeking inside some nearby tents. The first one is filled with sleeping bags and knapsacks, as is the second. Moving farther from the hub, we pull back the flap of this blue tent, and startle a couple in the midst of doing it.

"Sorry," we both say.

"We better listen first before going inside," I say.

At the next tent, all's quiet. Ducking inside, we find a circle of people meditating.

"This isn't working,' Candy says. "Let's ask around."

Since we both have work to do, we hug big time and agree to meet up for dinner. Glancing back at her as she sashays away, I wonder how I got so lucky.

GEOFFREY WITH A G

Thursday, August 14, 1969, late morning

"Are you Roberta?" I ask this plump chick, wearing a Jimi Hendrix T-shirt, who's sitting with this weaselly-looking guy about 20 with extra-long sideburns and a tattoo on his bicep that reads "Meg."

"Roberta? Who told you that? Roberta's gone," she says, smirking at her friend, both clearly wasted. "Phaedra has taken her place. Call me Roberta, and I'll ignore you, but try Phaedra and I may respond."

"I'm Mark. You have a little boy? Because there's this kid I've been trying to keep amused that keeps asking for his Mommy. He told me her name is Roberta. I asked around and someone said he's from the Peekskill commune and pointed me this way. So, like I said, are you Roberta?"

"He's right inside our tent resting," she says. Rushing into her tent, she comes back out looking panicked. "Where is he? I told him to stay here. He's going to get it."

"Well, he wandered over to the free kitchen. He's safe. My friend, Lanie, from my commune, got him. Good thing someone over there knows you. Your son's Jeff, right?"

"It's Geoffrey with a G. His father is Herbert with an H."

"I'm Bluebird, man," the guy says, clearly not wanting to be mistaken for the boy's father. He puts his hand out to slap me five, but I let it slide.

"Herbert resides in Scarsdale, along with all the other scar people," Phaedra says. "Right now, he's probably in his Wall Street office with the other wall people. That's what bankers do, you know, they develop scar tissue to hide their feelings and build walls around themselves."

"Let's go get Geoff," says her friend.

The roly-poly 6-year-old, is sitting on a blanket next to the kitchen eating a peanut butter and jelly sandwich and drinking some milk out of a plastic cup.

"We got a stash of kid food for occasions like this," says Lanie extending her hand to Geoffrey's mother.

"Mommy, where were you?" cries Geoffrey.

"Where was I? Where were you?"

"Where were you, Mommy? Where were you?"

"We're here now, little bro," Bluebird says. "And look at what you got. I wish I had some of that."

As we all walk back to their tent, my mind's working overtime. They're tripping. No wonder they lost the kid. They could lose him again and next time not be able to get him back so quickly.

"I'm with the Ohayo Mountain Family. We're partners with the Hog Farm," I start. "Look, I'm going around to the kitchens, fixing things that need fixing, like the shelves. I could sure use some help. You think Geoffrey could be my helper for a while?"

His mom gets it immediately. "Geoffrey, how would you like to be Mark's helper?"

Geoffrey looks me over and shrugs his shoulders, getting shoved off on others is nothing new for him.

"You know Lanie, the lady who gave you that sandwich? Well, she's a good friend of mine and I think she may have some other treats up her sleeve for you. I could use the help. What do you say?"

"You can take Buddy along," his mom offers. "He is all alone in the tent."

Geoffrey nods and goes inside, returning with a stuffed unicorn. So off we go, with his unicorn in one hand and mine in the other.

Growing up, I never really had much to do with younger kids, never was a camp counselor or anything like that, so I have no real explanation about how I developed this sense that allows me to empathize with children. But I have it. It's why becoming a teacher seems so right to me. Some people think working inside the system is a sell-out, but to me helping kids learn is easily as important as sitting around a commune rapping about the revolution. Anyway, Geoffrey's mom needs some time to get her act together, being with me will keep her son busy and safe.

At the kitchen, Lanie sits down and offers Geoffrey some raisins which he gobbles down, feeding some to Buddy the unicorn. Then she tells him this sweet story about a unicorn that rode on a rainbow. By now, he's cuddled into her.

I interrupt, saying we men have work to do. We go to a couple of the other make-shift kitchens and fix some stuff. I make sure he helps, even if it's to bang in a nail that's already been banged in.

After a while, he wants to go back to his mom. But when we get to their tent, Phaedra and Bluebird are gone.

"Let's wait here for them to come back. Y'know what? In September I'm going to be an elementary school teacher. I was thinking I better practice reading some kids' books. You got any?"

"How 'bout *The Cat in the Hat*?"

"Is that about that funny-looking guy around here who wears that straw cowboy hat?"

"No, silly. It's Dr. Seuss."

"Aren't you too young to be reading medical books?"

"No, silly. Wait. Wait here, I'll get it. Don't move."

Darting inside, he comes out with the book, which is one of my favorites.

We sit down on the grass and I read it to him. Then I read it again and, since he insists, I read it a third time.

"Boy, that cat in the hat can sure make a mess out of things," I say.

"Sometimes I pretend that it's their dad who comes home and not their mom."

"You must have a nice dad because you're such a nice boy."

"My daddy works a lot, but I miss him a ton. I haven't seen him since we moved to the new place."

"What's your last name?"

"Cabot. I'm Geoffrey James Cabot."

I make a mental note, Herbert Cabot in Scarsdale. After the festival, maybe I'll contact him to let him know where his son is.

Finally, his mom returns with some of her friends.

"Geoffrey, want to go swimming?" she asks.

"Can Mark come?"

"Hey, thanks, I gotta go—lots of other stuff to fix. See you all later."

"Thank you, so much," his mom says, giving me an unexpected hug.

"See you later, pal."

Geoffrey gives me a big hug too. As I stride up the hill, I ask the universe to please look after my new, young friend.

WHITE TIPI

Thursday, August 14, evening

Candy grins like the Cheshire cat when she spots me coming toward her. She's sitting at the fire pit with her San Francisco friends.

She's smiling just for you.

"I found us a place," she says.

"You're unbelievable, you know that."

"My friend Bonnie Jean said her and her old man have a big tipi to themselves and they'd be happy to share it."

"Share it?"

"Yeah, that's the best offer we have, and, it's just the two of them, not eight, like in my tent. How many are in yours?"

"I can't count that high."

Rob, Kasha's guy, passes me a pint of Southern Comfort.

"Where'd that come from?" I ask.

"The gods sent it. Knew we could use it."

Unlike two nights ago, when Candy and her crew wove rhythms around the moon, tonight everyone is just mellowing out. The festival starts tomorrow and we're all keenly aware that we need to conserve our energy.

Draping my arm around Candy's shoulder, I pull her close. She leans in without the slightest resistance.

As the night sky twinkles, Grayhawk stands and points out stars, planets, and constellations. Everyone swirls around on their butts trying to follow his extended arm.

A woman, wrapped in a day-glow sari, points toward Mars. "We all better be careful, 'cause the Red Planet's in retrograde."

People nod knowingly.

Candy taps me on the shoulder. "Let's get our stuff."

At her tent, people are asleep, so we move like cats gathering our belongings. Lifting my gear onto my back, I help hoist Candy's backpack onto her shoulders. She carries her drum in a duffel bag. Together, we amble over to a large, beautiful white tipi.

"Here we are. I'll go in first just to make sure it's OK." Returning quickly, she says, "It's cool, but they're going to sleep."

We set up our gear near the entrance. The other couple is on the far side. The woman is leaning over someone who's inside a sleeping bag. Walking toward us, she looks like a farmer's wife—erect posture, solid body, blond hair pulled back into a pony tail. She has a friendly, no-nonsense attitude.

With a tired smile, she extends her hand to me, "Hi, I'm Bonnie Jean. Pleased to meet you."

"I'm Mark, with the Ohayo Mountain Family. Thanks for letting us stay here."

"Appreciate all the help you and your commune are providing. Wavy's sick. I'm giving him some ginseng tea, which should help. Asking him to slow down is like asking the Red River to observe the Sabbath."

And with that she goes back to her man.

"Did she say Wavy, as in Wavy Gravy?" I ask.

"Of course. He's Bonnie Jean's husband. They're both incredible."

"Tomorrow will tell," I say, wishing I hadn't.

Zippering our sleeping bags together, we crawl inside. I say under my breath, "Couples are funny sometimes. She looks so straight, and he's like the king of the clowns."

"You know the song 'Girl from the North Country?'"

"Who doesn't?"

"Dylan wrote it about her."

PURR-FECT

Friday, August 15, 1969, morning

When we wake up, Bonnie Jean and Wavy Gravy are gone. Candy starts dressing.

"You did it," I say, resting on top of our sleeping bags. "We have a tent to ourselves."

"Groovy, right?"

"You put it out there and the universe said cool. Coincidence? I think not. But what befuddles me, my dear cosmic cutie, is why you're getting dressed, instead of getting undressed?"

"They could come back?"

"Doubt it. They're worker bees. They're out there buzzing away. Now Miss Sexy San Francisco, I emphatically recommend that for this very moment and many moments to follow, we take full advantage of our little playpen. Dost thou agree?"

"Purr-fect," she says, trilling her r's.

At first, there is the give and take of two. Candy's size and strength are a close match to my own. She stretches, sways, shimmies and shakes, synchronizing our bodies. Becoming excited and then frenzied, she's like a pinball machine way out of tilt, slinging me from bumper to bumper. Then we start merging, moving to the beat of a silent tom-tom, our bodies dissolving into a pulse that varies tempo, rhythm, and color. The only sound—our deep inhalations and spontaneous intonations. I lose me to we, then to something primal and cosmic. Opening my eyes for a second, her visage is one of uncontained joy. She's an angel. And me? I'm enchanted.

Fully spent, we hug, kiss, nuzzle, and snuggle. Crawling back into our sleeping bag, we fall back asleep completely entwined.

Voices awaken us.

"Wanna go see them set up?" someone asks.

"Starts this afternoon."

"It's finally here."

Where are we? Oh, yeah. I glance at Candy, her eyes peek out from the sleeping bag. We kiss trying to hold onto the magic, but our monkey minds are busily at work. Our kundalini energy rises like smoke up through the tipi's crown.

"Guess we should eat," she says, as she pecks me on my cheek.

At the free kitchen, Lanie and River are washing the breakfast pots.

"Anything left?" I ask.

A huge grin creeps over their faces. "A little birdy told me that you two definitely need some sustenance," Lanie says with a laugh.

We just smile.

"Well lookie here," continues River, "Lookie what your brother, River, found. How 'bout a bowl of granola and a cup of dee-licious instant coffee?"

"You two are dynamite," says Candy.

She feeds me from her spoon and I feed her from mine. Manny comes by and tells River and me he needs us for something, then a friend of Candy's calls to her and she gets up to go.

"Dinner time. OK?" I say.

"What fun," she whispers softly in my ear.

Although we've separated physically, she's right here inside me—her unselfconscious smile, soft blue eyes, those blond vertical pigtails, her feline body and unalloyed passion burrow into my soul.

"What fun," what did she mean by that? Fun? Why didn't she say that was absolutely incredible or I love you? Why just, what fun?

∽

Good thing I'm with River and Manny; maybe they'll help me sort it out.

"Look, I gotta talk to you cats. Candy and me just took the most cosmic, absolutely, totally insane, love-making trip ever.

The best. Man, it was psychedelic without the psychedelics, if you can dig it?"

"Brother, ain't you never been to California?" asks Manny.

River says. "Y'know that Beachboys' song "California Girls?" Well, whaddaya think they're singing about?"

"California? That's it?" I say "Are you for real? If all those West Coast chicks were like Candy, nobody, not a single fuckin' person in that whole fuckin' state, would ever get out of bed."

"She sounds like one of the Sirens," goes River.

"Definitely—a five-alarmer," I say.

"Learned about them in a Greek mythology class. They were these gorgeous babes, like mermaids, really, who used their mojo to lure sailors into deadly waters. They flipped out Odysseus so much he had to have his crew chain him up to keep him away from them."

"The Sirens were real," says Manny. "Canary Island chicks. They were smokin', man. Sailors would risk everything to get a little taste of what they were putting down."

"You saying Candy's leading me to destruction?"

They crack up. "Nah," River says. "Just talking about the magical spells some chicks can cast. It's alchemy."

"Should I go back to California with her?"

"Do what?" asks Manny.

"Move west?"

"Now wait a sec," says River, "I thought you said you were going to help save the world by becoming a teacher?"

"This could be the chance of a lifetime. How can I say no to that?"

"She asked you to move to San Francisco with her?" goes Manny.

"Not in so many words."

"Yeah, well, Mark, my man," River interjects. "What exactly did she say?"

"She didn't say nothin'. But what if she asks?"

"You got 'til Monday to figure that out," Manny tells me. "That's light years away from today."

SET AND SETTING

Friday, August 15, 1969, evening

I'm sitting with some of the Ohayo Mountain folks, as well as a few from our new West Coast family. We're all overwhelmed by the size of the crowd.

"Beyond far out," says Kasha, one of the main cooks.

"Farther out?" asks River with a smile.

"Beyond," says Rob.

"Beyonder beyond?" suggests one of Candy's friends.

"Any-whoo," says Lanie, "We're like Mother Hubbard—we got so many children, we don't know what to do."

"Where's all the fresh vegetables coming from anyway?" I ask. "Last night, you guys served corn, today cabbage soup. Where'd you get that stuff?"

"Lisa Law, that's how. She been going to all the local farms and buying anything and everything. She's a perpetual motion machine."

"Bless her," Kasha says.

"Bless you all," Candy responds.

She turns and kisses me. Then doing her best Mae West, she adds, "Brooklyn, is that a zucchini in your pocket or are you happy to see me?"

I blush a little, pull her to me, and kiss her back.

"OK, you two. You're gonna make everyone horny," goes River.

"I gotta show you something," Candy says, pulling my arm to get me up.

Walking away from the group, she opens her palm displaying two, bright purple pills. "You ever do Owsley's acid?"

"Once, it was incredible. But how do you know it's Owsley's? There a whole lot of bad acid going around."

" 'Cause he gave it to me."

"Gave it to you? How did he give it to you?"

"He's here and he gave it to me."

"He's here? I thought he was old?"

"I don't know how old he is, but wherever the Grateful Dead goes, the Bear goes. He's their soundman."

"Never knew that. The world's best psychedelic chemist is also the best soundman? Unbelievable. Guy is some kind of genius. He gave you those?"

"I know him from the Be-ins and the Trips Festival. So I got back stage and there he was. I mean, Mark, what the hell is this, the third degree?"

"I'm sorry, it's just that everything here seems so magical. That's all."

"He gave me two, one for me and one for you."

I take a deep breath. "You want to take them now?"

"When else? Everyone's tripping."

"Candy, I don't think I can do that."

"You afraid?"

"It's not that. For me doing acid is a spiritual experience."

"Me too."

"It's sacred, a sacrament. To do it right, the set and setting have to be just right."

Candy smiles at me. "We got each other."

"The right set means your mind is ready to leave your body; the right setting means you're in a place that's guaranteed safe. With my friends, most times, one of us doesn't trip just to make sure all the externals stay cool. That make sense?"

She's looking at the ground.

"I'm saying I don't want to trip in the middle of like a zillion people, where it's so chaotic. Let's save it for another time when we can do it right. Can you dig that?"

"Back home," she says, raising her voice, "the Pranksters, the Diggers, the Hell's Angels, all of us get together, drop acid, and cross over to the other side—partying, dancing, spacing out. When you're with cool people, things stay cool. Can you dig that?"

"Y'know, it's all just starting. Like Lisa Law said, 'we've gotta keep planting those peace seeds.' Taking a trip right here, right now, doesn't feel like the next right thing for me to do."

"I'm not in charge of the festival," Candy says. "I'm not in charge of you or anyone else. I'm in charge me. That's all. And if I want to trip, I trip."

"Do what you gotta do."

"I will." With that Candy turns and marches away.

THE PEOPLE'S STAGE

Friday, August 15, 1969, night

Watching Candy leave me is gut wrenching. I stand helpless. Walking by me, people keep their eyes averted. Maybe she'll change her mind. Maybe all the days of hard work, the nights of too little sleep, the pot, the booze, the heat took their toll. We'll straighten things out tomorrow.

If she's my soul mate, we'll get back together. If she isn't, I'm going to have to find a way to deal with that.

My fantasy of striking out for some new kind of life feels broken, beyond repair. Recalling my conversation with River and Manny, I think, *No, she didn't ask me to move to Haight-Ashbury with her.*

Dennis strolls past carrying his guitar. Seeing me he stops and asks what's happening. I tell him about what went down with Candy.

"I've been there, man. Nothing I can say, really. It's terrible, that's what, just fuckin' terrible."

"Terrible? I can handle terrible. This is excruciating."

Changing the subject, Dennis says, "I'm going to play tonight at the free stage they set up."

"Let me get this straight. We are at the biggest music festival ever and they're gonna to give it competition. Sounds like most things these wild men do—equally sensible and nonsensical."

"I wrote this new song. Would you listen to it and tell me what your think."

Finding a quiet spot, he sings "Down the Waterfall." It's about a guy who abandons his woman.

"Dennis, have some mercy, you're killing me dead."

"The lass is Maggie, my bride. She's in Brooklyn with our daughter, Erin. It breaks my heart that I left them."

"What's she like?"

"Aye, she's beautiful. From County Cork like me. We met in Brooklyn through mutual friends. Both of us moved to the

States to get away from our families. I landed a gig in a publishing house and she started going for a Master's degree. Everything was great. Then we had the baby, and I felt like I was trapped, suffocating. I just ran away. Ended up at the commune. I'm a coward, just like my old man."

"I was married."

"Like I say in the song, 'Husband means housebound and boozehound.'"

"Yeah, in unhappy marriages. You love her?"

"Can't stop thinking about my Maggie and our little girl."

"Maybe the universe is trying to tell you something. Look, I live in Brooklyn, too. If you go back, we can be friends."

Night has fallen. Back at the hub, people are sitting and standing in front of the ad hoc stage. Dennis heads over to join the line of performers. Naturally, first up is Wavy Gravy who plays "When the Saints Go Marching In" on a kazoo.

I look around hoping to see Candy's antennas bouncing above the crowd, but no such luck. Dennis comes on stage and introduces his song, "I have a wife and a daughter and I'm hoping to get back to them soon."

A few performers later, this woman with short dark hair takes the stage, tunes her guitar, and starts singing "Maid of Constant Sorrow." Two bars in is all it takes for all of us to recognize the gorgeous voice as Joan Baez's, the queen of folk music and the face of the protest movement.

"She's one of us," someone says.

I can't stand the uncertainty anymore, so I make a beeline to the white tipi. Light shines through the canvas. Opening the flap, I see Bonnie Jean is reading a book. My sleeping bag is there, but Candy's is gone. I want to ask Bonnie Jean where my Cal Conga Gal went, but she just nods toward me and continues reading.

Packing up my things, I say, "I'm going back to my tent. Thanks for sharing yours."

Joan Baez's voice resounds through the night. Getting into my sleeping bag, I keep track of my breathing, like Tom Law suggested, and it calms me down. I drift off to Baez singing "Any day now, I shall be released."

BAD TRIP TENT

Saturday, August 16, 1969, early morning

Upon awakening, my first thought is how can I get Candy back. Maybe I was wrong—maybe taking LSD here isn't the big deal I made it out to be. As my eyes plainly tell me, lots of people are spaced-out big-time. Sure, they're not too functional. But, what else is new? Maybe I was right—tripping here in the midst of all this chaos is asking for a bummer of epic proportions. Could she be freaking out somewhere and need my help?

Hoping to spot her, I circle the hub—no luck. Passing her tent, I pop my head in, but no one's there. If she had a truly terrible experience, she might be in the Bad Trip Tent.

Inside the tent are a dozen teeny boppers. Some are staring into space, a couple of others are talking to themselves. Several are curled up and sleeping. But no Candy.

Wearing their red pig armbands like Red Cross workers, Hog Farmers are attending to the kids. This cat I've seen around comes over to me. "Ohayo Mountain, right?"

"For sure."

"Here to help?"

Put on the spot, I say, "Um . . . yeah."

He surveys the scene and nods to his left. "See that kid over there in the cutoffs? He's been having a tough time. Whyn't you see what he needs?"

Taking a chair across from this small, tangled-haired, shirtless boy of about 15, I introduce myself. "I'm Mark, with the Hog Farm, what's going on?"

"Make it stop buzzing."

"Oh, that's just amp feedback. They're setting up for this band from Boston—Quill. Ever hear of 'em?"

"What? What? It's buzzing in here." he says, pointing to his head. "Make it stop."

"I know what that's like. Must have been some amphetamine in the acid you took. Just take it easy, it'll go away."

"What? You some kind of narc?" He looks around the large, noisy tent. "Where am I? In jail?"

"You're in a medical tent. We're here to help you."

"Help me? Oh Jesus. Help Me! Help me!" He holds his head with both hands.

"Some of the acid going around . . ."

"Who're you anyway? Try to bust me, and I swear, I'll fuckin' explode into little pieces all over you."

Quietly sliding onto a chair next to me, Wavy Gravy is grinning his gigantic, toothless grin.

"Hi, I'm Wavy. What's your name?"

"Kevin."

"Cool, Kevin."

"You a narc?"

"Narcs ain't allowed inside the festival. I'm with the Please Force. We're here to make everyone smile. You hear buzzing?"

"How'd you know?"

" 'Cause I just helped two other kids who took the brown acid and their heads were buzzing too. There's a tiny bit of speed in it."

"Make it stop."

"Kevin. Look at me. Look . . . right . . . at . . . me. Good. I'm going to do what worked with Sheila and Jose."

"What's that?"

"I'm going to sit right here with you and we'll wait for it to stop. I won't leave you until it does, and I'll make sure you're totally safe while we're waiting."

"Who are you?"

"I'm Wavy and right now the universe sent me to be your guardian angel, watching over you, keeping you safe. OK, Kevin?"

"I'm scared. Can you hold me?"

"Yes, indeed."

Opening his arms wide, he gently pulls Kevin to him. Recognizing me, the Hog Farm leader and my former tipi mate, nods and smiles, not in a hipper-than-thou way, but in a friendly how-do-you-do gesture. He mouths to me, "You're beautiful, thanks."

Wavy Gravy reminds me of Max, the boy from *Where the Wild Things Are*, who tames all the wild monsters by staring, without blinking, into the yellow of their eyes. Wavy Gravy's focus, his positive peaceful vibe and unrelenting fortitude have kept this festival together.

Leaving the tent, I realize that Candy represents the last opportunity to deep-six my teaching plans and take off on some kind of life-changing, fantasy voyage. Whatever illusion I had about us, I better try to leave on the river bank of my memory and paddle on.

ON OUR SIDE

Saturday, August 16, 1969, late morning

The whop-whop-whop of a helicopter has become a familiar sound. That's the way bands are being ferried in and out. But looking up, we see this helicopter has "US Army" stenciled on its side.

Along the path, people freeze and stare.

"What the hell is happening?" asks a tall girl wearing a T-shirt emblazoned with a clenched fist.

Someone says, "Looks like they're sending in the army."

"Told ya," a thin black guy goes. "The Man's gonna shut this shit down. Gettin' too heavy for 'em."

"Word's out that Woodstock's working and the straights are scared," the tall girl offers.

"Yeah, they gotta be thinking, what's next?" this other chick says.

Watching the helicopter fly by, a guy with a buzz cut says, "Man, one Huey ain't gonna do it. I know, I been to 'Nam. They'd need hundreds of choppers and thousands of troops to stop this festival."

"Wait and see, bro," the black guy tells him.

I jog the rest of the way to the hub where everyone is excited. "What's up?" I ask Kasha.

"Governor Rockefeller declared us a disaster area. So the National Guard's bringing in supplies."

"That better be all they have in mind," her boyfriend Rob says.

"Cool out, baby. They're using helicopters, 'cause the roads are useless. What do you suggest—the subway?"

"Dan the Man came by and told us about it. He rounded up a bunch of folks and took them to the other side of that hill," Bonnie Jean says pointing.

"Let me get this straight," says the black guy. "The National Guard's coming to help us?"

"We're American citizens, aren't we?" she replies.

"If it comes from Dan, it's probably true," Rob says. Others nod in agreement.

"Once they unload the supplies, they'll start bringing them this way," Kasha continues, "and we'll sort it all out."

The whop-whop-whop resumes as the aircraft lifts off. A few minutes later, our people come rushing over the rise hauling all sorts of containers. There are bags and bags of sandwiches, bottles of water galore, canned goods by the case, sacks of rice and oatmeal, bushels of fruit and vegetables, boxes of first aid supplies, cardboard cartons filled with yellow inflatable pup tents.

"We all held hands in a huge circle, so the pilot knew where to set down," River tells us. "It was totally wild. Another one is on its way. As soon as we hear it, we gotta race back and be a human landing pad again."

"Perishables first," shouts Lanie into a bullhorn. "Bring the sandwiches and the fruit to the kitchens."

Kasha takes the bullhorn and pushes the buzzer: "People. Listen to this." Holding a piece of paper, she reads, " 'Enjoy these sandwiches. The members of the Women's Auxiliary of the Monticello Jewish Community Center made them for you. We didn't want you to go hungry. Stay healthy, be safe. God bless you.' "

We all cheer.

Tom Law takes the horn. "The National Guard did this for us. One of the G.I.'s said they wished they could stay, especially for Hendrix. Y'know Jimi was a paratrooper. Man, they're on our side."

More cheers. Word spreads fast, and in no time the hub is teeming with folks looking for food and water. Just as with breakfast, a dozen lines form almost instantly. Everyone knows the drill: Injured people go first, then grown-ups with children. No skipping, no pushing, just keep moving forward. We'll share whatever we have.

Taking a moment, I ask Kasha if she's seen Candy.

"She's around here somewhere," Kasha says.

"She OK?"

"Candy? She's better than OK, she's groovy."

"That's great. She a great person. Thanks."

I do a slow 360, but can't locate anyone with pigtail antennas. A second helicopter circles overhead and the landing pad people split. When they return, the supplies are divvied up, this time with some people getting off the food lines to help out.

Manny shows up and I tell him about the pup tents.

"Supposed to rain, so let's hand them out," I say.

We each grab a carton containing a dozen tents. Before going over the ridge, we each take one for ourselves, just in case. On the way down, we ask people if they have any shelter. If they say no, we hand them a tent. Simple.

But as the dark clouds signal, it won't stay simple for long.

CREEDENCE

Saturday, August 16, 1969, midnight

I'm bopping down Groovy Way when I bump into Manny who's with two straight-looking women. One's slightly taller than he is, with a dark pageboy, cute upturned nose and long limbs; the other is plump, also with short hair, and a ready smile. He introduces me. The taller one is Pam; the other's either Judy or Julie. They go to NYU nursing school and are here as volunteers. Manny met Pam in the medical tent where she bandaged up his finger after he sliced it with a utility knife.

"I'm on the way to catch some music. Wanna come?" I ask.

"We can get into the press section," Manny says.

"How?"

"If we show them this," says Manny as he ties the red cloth with the hog insignia on his right arm, "they're supposed to let us in."

"Where's the press section?" Pam asks.

"Right smack dab in front of the stage."

"Would they let us in too?"

"Sure thing, you're volunteers too."

We take our time wending our way to the stage. The first stop is at the neverending lines for the Port-O-San. Next, since we're all hungry, we go to the medical tent, behind which there is a buffet of sorts for the doctors and nurses. Pam and her friend go inside to make sandwiches for all of us to share.

Waiting for their return, Manny goes, "Look, it's me and Pam, OK?"

"Yeah, sure. All I can think about is Candy."

"Dennis told me. Sorry, man. You got to let it go."

"Manny, it's only been a day."

"Out here, a day's like a week, know what I'm saying?"

"Still, a week's not too long to be hurting for such a super fine chick."

"Me and Pam, OK?"

"Is her friend Judy or Julie?"

"One or the other."

The girls return and the four of us walk hand in hand down to the stage. A wall of eight-foot-tall plywood sheets runs the length and sides of the stage. It serves as the outer wall of the press section and as a buffer between the audience and the performers. We go along it until we find an entrance.

Feedback crackles as the stage crew changes over from one band to the next. Strutting over to this very large individual in a staff shirt, Manny says, "We're Hog Farmers and nurses."

"Who?"

Pointing to his arm band, Manny says, "This allows us to catch the show from the press section."

"Who told you that?"

Manny looks like he wants to deck the guard, a decidedly bad idea. I step in. Moving between the two of them, I say, "Hey, man, look, you guys are doing a dynamite job keeping the music flowing and we're doing a dynamite job keeping the scene cool. Without you and without us, this place would be a fucking insane asylum. Dig it?"

"Kind of hard to hear. Hog Farm? Cool. Go on in."

I slide my hand behind me and Manny gives me five.

"Who's playing?" asks Pam.

"Grateful Dead just finished. Creedence is up next."

"Judy and I are crazy about them."

The press section is half-empty. On the left side are the press people, identifiable by their cameras and notebooks. On the right side, there's people from the hub, including Rob and Kasha.

"How were the Dead?" Manny asks.

"I hate to say this, but they sounded tired," replies Rob.

Probably messed up on Owsley acid, I say to myself.

"I hope Creedence puts on a good show," Pam says.

"To me, they're just a Top 40 group," Kahsa says.

"Not so quick," I say. "They're getting our message across. Take 'Proud Mary'—all about how reefer makes people mellow and giving."

"Or 'Fortunate Son,'" says Manny, backing me up. "Tells it like it is. Working stiffs are the ones fighting in 'Nam, while all the rich folks are making money hand over fist and getting their kids draft deferments."

"I like their name, Creedence," Rob goes. "They tell the truth, not like our government which lies, lies, lies."

This little dose of reality hits us all hard and we retreat into silence, watching the roadies set up. Manny has his head in Pam's lap and she strokes his hair gently. Judy and I lie next to each other.

Finally, standing above us on stage, not ten feet away, is John Fogerty. Clean-shaven, hair coiffed just so, wearing tight jeans, a blue cowboy shirt, and a brown, fringed suede vest, he's strumming his guitar and peering into the darkness, like he's trying to see if there's anyone still awake. Some guy from way back hollers, "John, we're with you." And that's all Fogerty needs to crank up his group and let it fly.

The band does the first four songs note for note like their records. I feel like calling up to them to rock out, but instead Pam and Judy keep shouting, "We love you."

This is music you can count on. Like Bach's fugues or Miles's solos, they are sonic gems—uplifting, potent, flawless. I bet a hundred years from now, people will be humming along to Bach, nodding their heads to Miles, and singing "Big wheel keep on turning."

Manny says something to Pam, she turns and they kiss. At the commune, he told me he's a one-woman man, and no woman there turned him on. Maybe Pam's the one.

Judy and I sway back and forth, taking in the music and enjoying the summer night.

After the set, we walk the girls back to their tent. While we talk for a bit, a couple of other nurses pass by and say hello.

Then Pam whispers something to Judy who smiles, hugs her, then pecks Manny and me on the cheek and heads inside.

The lovebirds, arms wrapped around each other, walk away, singing, "Suzie Q, I love you, my Suzie Q."

WATER TRUCK

Sunday, August 17, 1969, morning

Since he asked, I decide to check in with Dan the Man. Outside his office, several workers are milling around. Dan opens his door and scans the scene. He stops when he sees me. "Just the man I'm looking for."

"Me?"

"If I wasn't so full of crap," he says, "here's what I would have said, 'There's that dependable cat Mark. He can fill in for that no-show bastard.'"

"I can sub. What's up?" I reply.

"Ever drive a flatbed?"

"Yeah. When I worked construction in Brooklyn, sometimes I drove the truck that carried the pneumatic drills and compressors. What you got?"

Pointing, he says, "We got a flatbed with a water tank on it. I need you to drive it up the hill, stopping along the way, so people can get water."

"Up the hill, through the crowd? You serious?"

"Who's got time to joke? We planted those people in that field. Now we gotta water 'em."

"Can't Mohammed come to the mountain?"

"Don't work. It'd get way too crowded here. We gotta bring the mountain to them."

He ducks inside. Re-emerging, he flips me the keys, then surveys the sky. "Let's get it done now, before the rain shuts us down."

I stutter in response, but he puts up his hand, goes back in and comes out with some bread and cheese, a bottle of Coca-Cola and a couple of cigarettes. "This is all I got. OK, man?"

"Just need to look it over, figure it out," I say, but Dan's already walking off with a work crew.

How am I going to drive up that hill without killing people?

Climbing inside, I see the truck has a four-speed transmission, with a high range/low range option. Better to use low range, it'll keep the action sure-footed, allowing me to roll up the hill without stalling. With my right foot on the brake pedal, I engage the emergency brake. Pushing in the clutch with my left foot, I slide through the gears. I turn the key, the engine kicks over instantly, and the gas tank reads half-full.

Leaning out of the window, I ask one of the security guys to check out the brake lights and turn signals. I honk the horn, which makes a couple of people jump. What else? Oh, yeah. Climbing down from the cab, I check the tires. The water tank is modeled on a cow's teats with six hoses attached. I loosen a couple of taps and water comes streaming out. The truck's A-OK.

Back behind the wheel, I move the seat forward adjust my side-view mirror, then slide over and adjust the one on the right side. There's a tightness in my chest. I tell myself to breathe.

Shit, this is scary. No room for mistakes, but I don't dwell on that. Fear is the fastest route to failure. The first time I drove that construction truck on Brooklyn streets, I told myself I could do it and I did. Same here. People need water. Here's a water truck. I'm gonna drive it.

There is one more thing. I lock up the truck and amble up the hill, scanning the crowd. I spot a group of teenagers, three boys and three girls, laughing at something a shirtless, muscular guy just said.

One of the girls raises her middle finger to him.

"Ernie, say that again and I'm gonna hafta kick your ass."

"This I gotta see," Ernie says.

"The both of us will do it," goes this other girl.

Walking over, I say, "Hey bro."

"Hey, what's up?" Ernie replies.

"I'm with the Hog Farm, name's Mark. I need a solid. See that truck over there. I got to drive it up the hill to get water to our brothers and sisters. Dig it?"

"Need some help, huh?"

"You got it, my man," I say and slap him five.

Ernie introduces me to James and Devon. I repeat their names to myself so I won't forget them. The girls tell me their names, but I make sure to seem uninterested in them. I need help not trouble.

"With all these freaks everywhere," Devon asks, "how we gonna do it?"

"How the fuck indeed? Here's my idea. How 'bout you all run interference for me. I'll drive as slow as possible while you go ahead shooing people out of the way."

"Let's surround the truck," one of the girls suggests. "Some in front, some on the sides and some in the back."

"How far up you planning on going?"

"I don't know. Maybe three or four stops, until we get to the top. Safety is number one. In this game, we can't make a single error."

"Everyone's plenty thirsty," Ernie says.

"You can't leave me, not for a second."

They look at each other. "What's there to think about?" says James. "I'm gonna get some more of our friends."

When the whole gang is assembled, I say, "You're good people, y'know that."

"Not one of us is ever going to forget we did this, not ever," Ernie says.

They divide themselves into four groups, with Ernie leading the way, James and this other guy, Colin, keeping an eye on the sides and Devon taking up the rear.

"It's show time," I shout.

Turning on the engine, I slide the transmission lever into low range and the gear shift into first. Moving as slowly as possible, honking as I go, we travel about half a football field before Ernie puts up his hand for me to stop.

In no time, we've got long lines spreading out from the truck. When they start dwindling, I honk my horn, get a thumbs-up from Ernie, James, Devon, and Colin, crawl to the next stop, repeat the process, and crawl forward until we're at the crest of the hill.

The sky is getting darker. The winds are picking up. Chip Monk, the stage announcer, implores everyone to get down from the huge speaker towers that are starting to sway.

With my crew's help, I make a slow U-turn and head back down, stopping three more times. At the next to the last stop, I'm to the left of the stage.

Wavy Gravy is holding the microphone. He's jubilant. "What we have in mind is breakfast for four hundred thousand. It's not just the Hog Farm. It's the Ohayo Mountain Family, the Pranksters, and all the volunteers who put in their time, who set up the free kitchens. We're feeding each other. We must be in heaven, man."

Clapping and cheers ripple through the pasture.

The Hog Farm, the Ohayo Mountain Family, the Pranksters—that's us, that's me. How do you like them apples?

My eyes mist up. I'm proud of what we've accomplished. I'm proud of myself.

Wavy continues, "Move through the forest to the Hog Farm, we have 17 lines in place."

Returning to the construction office, my escorts give me the peace sign and head back to their spot on the hill.

I hand in the keys. Dan pats my back. "Knew you could do it. Two days down, one to go. We all gotta keep on truckin'."

ROBERTA

Sunday, August 17, 1969, afternoon

I spot Roberta, Geoffrey with a G's mom, but pass by without saying anything. The last time I saw her was Thursday, when I walked away pissed off at her failure to keep track of her young son. There's a tap on my arm.

"Hello again, remember me?" she says.

"You're Roberta, right? Geoffrey's mom? Wait, you gave yourself a new tag, Hydra or something."

"Phaedra. But I'm OK with Roberta. Last time I was pretty high."

"You and half a million others."

"You were judging me and I didn't dig it."

"Hey, you're doing your thing, right?" I say.

"Here I am trying to talk with you and you're spouting slogans."

"Look, I know the drill. I'm supposed to act like everything's always cool, but I'm no good at pretending. To me, some things are definitely uncool. Like war, like prejudice and violence. And like not taking care of our kids."

"Just so you don't get any ideas, Geoffrey's at the playground with my friend Cathy and her daughter. Look, life changed really fast for me, can you understand that?"

"Uh-huh."

"I graduated from Barnard, majored in anthropology."

"Roberta, you don't have to tell me . . ."

"I want you to understand. I won a scholarship to study at Oxford."

"In England?"

"Of course, in England. That's where I met Herbert. He was an economics major. Things were great, we got married, Geoffrey came along and we moved to the States where Herbert had a connection at a big Wall Street firm."

"Roberta, let me say this again: None of this is my business."

"It is your business. We're all each other's business. We're in this thing together. I mean you're with the Hog Farm, right?"

"Well, actually, I came here with the Ohayo Mountain Family, outside of Woodstock, just up the road from your commune in Peekskill. But after this, I'm going back to Brooklyn. I've got a job lined up as an elementary school teacher that I'm probably going to take."

"No wonder you were so good with Geoffrey."

"Thanks."

"Well, Herbert started earning big money, really big money, packaging financing deals for major corporations. We moved out of our apartment in Queens and bought a house in Scarsdale."

"Fancy-pants land."

"Last Christmas, his firm sponsored an opening at MOMA, and I met this Venezuelan artist, Juan. We spent some time together at his studio on Bank Street in the West Village. Then one day, it was April Fools' Day, Herbert was away on a business trip and Juan turned me on to LSD. It was like taking a truth serum. I looked in a mirror and wondered: Who's that person staring back at me?"

"Yeah, my first trip was something else."

"So you get it. When I got back home I paid the babysitter, then I went into Geoffrey's room and sat gazing at him. He's so adorable, so precious. I kissed him and kissed him. I love him so much. I roamed around the house wondering who lived here. All these fabulous furnishings—whoever it was, it certainly wasn't the Roberta and Herbert who met in England and fell in love. No, they were gone. It was someone else's house. I didn't belong here."

"You talk to Herbert?"

"Did we ever talk? Mark, when you do what he does, when every deal involves millions and millions of dollars, little things like your wife's feelings or your kid missing you, seem tiny, inconsequential."

"But, for Geoffrey's sake . . ."

"I kept on looking at my beautiful son and thinking unless I do something, he's going to become Herbert. I couldn't live with that. At the health food store, I met some people from the Peekskill People's Commune and we clicked."

"Look, I know I got an attitude. But your son has rights too. He told me he never sees his dad. Unless Herbert did something terrible to him, you don't have any right to keep them away from each other."

"I hear you."

"Listen, Roberta, you're a brave person. Maybe there's something you can do with that anthropology degree. You're in charge of you, not Herbert, and not that idiot I saw you with. So take charge."

She stretches out her arms. I hesitate a moment. She's right, understanding does change things. We hug.

"Hey can you wait just a minute? I have something for Geoffrey." Trotting to my tent, I grab the yellow pup tent I was planning on keeping for myself. "Please give this to him. He'll dig it."

WITH A LITTLE HELP

Sunday, August 17, 1969, afternoon

I'm listening to two guys playing guitar and banjo, when this chick, short hair, coral blue eyes, wearing a tank top that looks like it's painted on, sits down next to me. "Hi, remember me?"

"I gotta answer your question with a question. Would you leave if I said no or am I better off lying?"

"I'm Joanie and you're cute," she laughs. "I met you last night outside the nurses tent. I'm friends with Pam and Judy."

"First off, you win the cute prize. And second, last night was a long time ago. Like my main man Manny says, a day here is like a week."

"Manny, Manny, Manny, that's all Pam talked about all day."

"He's good people. Solid as a locomotive."

"How about you? You good people?"

"It depends. Manny gets along with everyone. Me, I get along best with people I have respect for. The others? Not as much. People tell me I'm too serious."

"Me, too. What a weekend."

"Festival's been amazing. Manny and me came here last Monday with the Ohayo Mountain Family and we've been busting our asses helping to keep this thing going. Of course, not just us, and, y'know what, so far it's worked. You nurses have been working real hard, too."

"Thanks. Catch much music?"

"Saw Creedence Clearwater Revival last night."

"Who's on today?"

"Everyone who didn't play yesterday or Friday. But I got no idea who that is. All I know is that Hendrix is up last."

"I hear the music starting up. Want to go listen?"

I get up, extending my hand to help her up. She allows herself to be pulled up against my chest, lingers for a moment before leaning back on her heels.

We stop at the crest overlooking the stage. While I could probably finesse our way back into the press section like I did last night, it doesn't feel right. Once is enough. Moving through the crowd, we sit down maybe a football field away.

Onstage, the band is finishing up a song. The lead singer has on a long-sleeved, tie-dyed T-shirt.

"Who's playing?" I ask a girl seated next to us.

"Joe Cocker."

We shrug our shoulders.

"He's English," the girl continues and passes us a joint.

The band starts playing "Just Like a Woman." Cocker sings the opening line "Nobody feels any pain" and he sounds like he's an alumni of the Ray Charles School of Singing, and like Brother Ray, he sings behind the beat. While Dylan's original is a scornful picture of a former lover, Cocker's full-bodied voice tells a tale of a heart filled with anguish. The music takes him away. Us too.

Joanie and I exchanges smiles, she leans against my chest. I put my arms around her shoulders, drawing her head alongside mine, tousling her hair.

The organ plays two notes, and a murmur undulates through the crowd. We all know this one. It's "With a Little Help from My Friends," from *Sergeant Pepper*, a record I bet every single person here owns and knows by heart.

Unlike the little ditty that Ringo croons, Cocker sings as if his life depends on it. He wails the lyrics incoherently, whirling his right arm playing an invisible guitar, staggering, vibrating, almost collapsing, then resurrecting himself. He's testifying, telling it like it is: "I get by with a little help from my friends."

A little help from my friends? I'm hip. Cocker's turning the Beatles' song into an anthem. It's about all of us here at Woodstock. How has everyone gotten through all the bummers—the chaos, traffic jams, thunderstorms, the hunger, the heat, all the rotten conditions? How? With a little help from our friends—a shared sandwich here, a laugh, a sip of water there, a toke, a free meal, a smile, a kiss, a hug.

When Joe Cocker finishes, people rise to their feet and pump their fists in the air. And, as if on cue, the skies go from gray to black. Storm clouds rush in. One upon another, lightning bolts flash like strobes—freezing the crowd's upturned heads, open mouths, outstretched arms, and then thunderclaps explode and torrential rain renders our bowl-shaped metropolis once more a flooded city.

"Here we go again," I say, grabbing Joanie's hand. "Let's move quick."

Running up the hill, we approach this couple who are moseying down like nothing's happening. The guy is very tall and bearded, but it's the chick who catches my eye, because she's got two pigtails sticking straight up. We exchange a sideways glance. Could it have been only a couple of days ago that I fantasized about moving to San Francisco to be with Candy?

I lead Joanie to where the school buses are parked. Pulling open the door of the Ohayo Mountain bus, we go inside. It's empty. At the back is a built-in bed with covers on it. The rain is slowing down and a band of grey clouds illuminate the interior.

"Our ark," I say.

"It's neat," Joanie says. Taking a blanket, she turns her back to me, takes off her soaking clothes and wraps herself in it. I grab another cover and do the same.

"OK, I'm going to be a nurse, I have to get this out of the way. Anyway, I'm on birth control and I don't have any venereal diseases. How 'bout you?"

"Not now, not ever. No lice, no VD. Hey, Joanie, I'm glad you're asking. I ask too."

"You're not angry?"

"I've been around the block a couple of times and I can tell you I don't think all you need is love."

"Good, now that's out of the way. One more thing . . ."

I put my finger on her lips. "Let's find that place before there were words."

She nods.

We stretch out and I pull her close and we kiss deeply, melting into each other. Our arms and legs magnetically attracted, entwining us.

Embracing again, we start making love, moving frenetically, passionately, wildly like broncos. After a while, our vibe mellows. We're descending on a cloud, drifting down to earth. Holding each other close, we fall asleep intertwined in each other's arms. The yellows, crimsons, violets, and indigos of the setting sun flow through the bus's front window, as we slowly regain consciousness.

"Is the storm over?" she asks.

"Looks like it's clearing, but no guarantees."

"I have to go. I'm working tonight."

"What a shame. I'll walk you."

Getting dressed, we smile and hug and kiss and smile and hug and kiss some more, until we stumble out the door and onto the grass.

"Mark, you're so sweet."

"Hey, you better cut that out. I got my reputation to consider."

She looks away. "I don't want to, but I have to tell you something. I have a fiancé, he's in med school. He was supposed to come here with me, but at the last minute the hospital called him in."

Blood rushes from my head. I'm wobbly on my feet. Leaning back against the bus, I steady myself to regain my composure. "Funny, I was just gonna tell you, I'm dating an X-ray machine. It's kind of tough though, 'cause it can see right through me."

She looks flustered. "I didn't come here to meet anyone. But seeing everyone being so free, I started thinking about how I'm getting married. Married. Sounds like a death sentence, doesn't it?"

"I was married once and I survived."

"But you're so nice, and we clicked, and, well, this could be the last time for me, with someone else."

"Joanie, it's OK. No, better than OK. What just happened was magical. I feel like we've known each other forever. You're so beautiful. But this is Woodstock. It was only built to last for a weekend. Know what I'm saying?"

"It was magical."

"One more thing, because real life can get real complicated, I want you to know that what went down between us, stays here," I say, touching my chest. "Like the song says, 'Ain't nobody's business but our own.'"

"You are sweet."

"What a lucky guy Mr. Med School is." Coming to the top the hill, I stop. "You better go the rest of the way by yourself."

She gives me a quick kiss and jogs away.

Glaring at the heavens, I shout, "This is not funny."

But maybe in its own way it is. There's a message here for me. It's important to be willing to change, but so is being steadfast to what you truly believe. Being serious doesn't mean not laughing at my own absurdity. Yeah, pain is part of life, but so is love. In the past four days, the universe let me be in love with two beautiful women. What more could I ask?

JIMI

Monday, August 18, morning

"It's over. Long live Woodstock," I say to Rob as he and Kasha sit down for a peanut. butter and jelly sandwich breakfast.

"Sounds like they're playing *Electric Ladyland* over the PA," says Rob.

"It's not the PA," says a guy from one of the other communes. "It's Hendrix live. He's on stage now."

"Now?" Rob asks, looking around. "I don't normally talk like this, but it's Monday morning."

"Honey, just think of it as very, very late Sunday night," Kasha says.

"They said Hendrix plays last. I guess last is now," I say.

"Probably the only thing all weekend that's happening as planned," goes Lanie.

"If Hendrix is playing there, what are we doing here?" asks Rob.

With that everyone rises to go to the pasture. Everyone but me. I'm exhausted and kind of bummed out.

"Aren't you comin'?" River asks.

"Nah. I've had enough excitement. I'm gonna just take it light and stay here."

The hub is mellow. A mother plays with her baby, a woman in an Indian print dress interprets Tarot cards for two chicks, a guy resting against a tree reads *Autobiography of a Yogi*, a girl plays her guitar softly.

Wondering if Joanie and I left anything on the O.M.'s school bus last night, I go to the parking area. "Further," the Pranksters' bus that Tom Wolfe celebrated in *The Electric Kool-Aid Acid Test*, is here along with other psychedelically painted vehicles. I try to imagine what it would be like to travel cross-country in one of them. I have to admit they're too conspicuous for me. This Brooklyn boy likes his privacy.

Without thinking and without knocking, I open the bus door and go inside. Lifting his head from the bed, Clark peers at me and nods. Alongside of him, this cute young thing I recognize from Candy's drumming circle lifts her head too.

"Sorry, I was here last night and was checking I didn't leave anything," I say.

"That's cool, Mark, ain't nobody here but us chickens," Clark says.

"Cool, man. See ya."

That's Clark for you.

Darlene, another friend of Candy's, is playing roly-poly with Spring, her toddler daughter.

"Totally far out weekend," Darlene says. "Can you imagine, my baby has all this imprinted on her brain? Her whole head must be filled to the brim with all the love and joy that surrounded us here."

"I'd love to meet your daughter in like 15 years and find out what she remembers."

As we're talking, this longhaired guy carrying an unusual camera passes us heading toward a lean-to.

"Hendrix done?" I ask.

"Just finished. He's amazing."

"The best," I say.

"That cat has reimagined the electric guitar."

"Reminds me of Coltrane."

"I can dig it. Two geniuses. Hey, you want to see the show?"

"See the show? What do you mean?"

"This is a video camera. It's the newest thing. Uses videotape not film. No developing, just shoot it and show it."

"I saw something on videotape and it was like real," says Darlene.

"Just going to load up the player to see what I got. You're welcome to join me."

We jump up. Taking Spring's hand, her mother asks, "Can we see it, too?"

"No problem, just keep her back from the equipment," he replies.

Inside the lean-to it's dark, the only light comes from a small screen that a curly haired woman is watching.

"Hey, Peter, what did you get?"

"Ellen, I got Mr. Jimi Hendrix."

"Dynamite."

Peter drops down in front of some equipment, pops out the tape Ellen had on and pops in the one from his camera.

Jimi Hendrix appears on the screen. Darlene's right, it looks real. Peter's vantage point is a little ways up the hill, just beyond the press section. Hendrix is wearing a red headband, a white, fringed, beaded vest, and large diamond ear studs, which reflect the sunlight toward the camera and the crowd.

"The world's hippest cat," I say.

"And the most beautiful," says Darlene.

"You can say that again," says Ellen.

"You gotta see this," says Peter, as he skips through the tape.

He stops it at a point where Hendrix is playing the refrain from "Voodoo Child." He explores every sonic nuance of an electric guitar, incorporating feedback, distortion, note bending into rock, blues, and R&B riffs, creating music that is at once of this world and out of it.

For a few notes into his next number, his bassist plays along, but then he cedes the stage to the master. Hendrix launches into the "Star-Spangled Banner." He begins with a jazzy riff, but, when he gets to the part that goes "and the rockets' red glare," Jimi breaks free from the War of 1812. His wailing guitar brings the song into 1969, into the midst of a firefight in the Mekong Delta—the whop-whop-whopping of choppers, the brat-a-ta-ting of machine guns, the blasting of mortars and, above it all, the shrill screams of wounded and dying soldiers, all ricocheting through the swamps. When he gets to "that our flag was still there," he segues into "Taps." Yeah the flag's still there, motherfucker, but what about the soldiers? For them, caught in its jaws, war is hell on earth.

In this darkened space, lit only by a small television set, we stand stunned, minds blown. Hendrix is telling the truth, the counterculture's simple message: let's stop killing each other, let's learn to live together.

The tape continues. Hendrix plays a couple of more tunes, mellowing things out, ending with his first hit "Hey, Joe." Raising his right hand toward the sky, he intones, "Goodbye, everybody." Jimi Hendrix, the headliner, brought it home.

Three Days of Peace and Music ends on day four.

AMIGOS

Monday, August 18, 1969, late morning

Three Days of Peace and Music, that's what the organizers said would happen and that's what they delivered. Also, they promised Max Yasgur they'd return his land to its pre-festival condition. Maybe not so fast.

Under cloudless skies, standing a short way up from the stage, I turn in a circle watching the last wave of concertgoers depart. What a scene of devastation the hundreds of thousands of fellow stoned, beautiful, righteous freaks have left behind. Embedded in the muck, among so many other things, are broken tambourines and transistor radios, ripped dayglow boas and ballet slippers, empty Chianti bottles and Styrofoam coolers, and an assortment of discarded hookahs and pipes.

But not all of it is tossable. Clothing, blankets, camping equipment lie in state, just needing to be excavated from the mud and cleaned up to be used again.

One thing is obvious, much of what made it in never made it out. It was simpler for the huge crowd to abandon their things than trying to carry or drag their funky, filthy belongings miles back to where most of them left their cars.

"We're supposed to clean this up?" some guy asks. "Are they serious?"

"We can only do what we can do in the time we have to do it," Lisa Law says "Hugh, Bonnie Jean, Tom, and the rest of us are flying back to New Mexico tomorrow night."

"Pranksters start driving west first thing Wednesday morning," Kasha says.

"They hired demolition and garbage companies to finish it up," Tom Law says.

"One good thing," Rob adds, "they're letting us keep all the kitchen equipment we can fit on our buses."

Large plastic garbage bags are handed out to aid in the cleanup. I work half-heartedly adding my bags to the heaps of trash and placing salvageable things in piles.

I'm homesick. For the first time in weeks, I have this over-whelming desire to be back in Brooklyn, in my apartment, in my bed, my refrigerator stocked, the sun shining through the windows, the Brooklyn Botanic Gardens a block away and Pros-pect Park right across the street.

I join Manny, and side by side we pull all sorts of junk out of the muck. I claim a rust-colored, fringed, suede jacket and a pair of tan boots. Manny finds a black Stetson, dunks it in water and puts it on his head.

"Hey, you look like the real thing."

"Just what the world needs, a Puerto Rican cowboy from the Bronx."

"What's happening with you and Florence Nightingale?"

"Pam and me fell hard for each other. After Creedence, we walked all over the place, visiting other camping areas, sitting by the pond, and the whole time, you know what, we talked and talked. Never did that before. If I said something, she said 'I know.' Every time she told me how she felt about something, I said, 'That's how I feel.' "

"Manny, that's beautiful."

"Pam's amazing: no bullshit, no games, no girly-girly stuff, totally real."

"So what's gonna happen?"

"Gotta go for it. I'm going back to the commune, pack up my things and move to her place in Queens. She and Judy share an apartment."

"Judy cool with it?"

Manny nods. "She said it's OK for now."

"What'll you do in the city?"

"Get a job, what else? But Pam's talking about me getting my GED. She thinks I could become a radiologist. Mark, tell me the truth, can you see me in college?"

"Hey, my man, definitely. You're smart. If you don't bullshit around and just do the work, college ain't that hard. Finding your soulmate, now, that's hard."

"She thinks ahead. I like that."

River and Lanie wander over. "We hardly got to hang out with you guys during the festival."

"Busy, busy bees," I say.

"Absolutely fantastic," says Lanie.

"We got to know a lot of Hog Farmers," River says. "We dig them. They're serious about creating an alternative community."

"They're good people," says Manny, "Hardworking, serious, and a gas to be around."

"Far as I'm concerned," I say, "You can't be a revolutionary if someone else is paying the rent or sending you money."

"Or if the men only do men's work and the women do all cooking and cleaning," adds Lanie.

"Nothing against the Ohayo Mountain Family," River goes. "But the Hog Farm is where it's at."

"Bonnie Jean invited us to fly back to New Mexico with them," Lanie adds.

"What'd you say?" asks Manny.

"Lisa Law is talking about starting a yoga school. Maybe becoming holistic healers. They've been studying with this Shaman."

"It's what we always talked about. We got to give it a try," River says. "What's up with my brothers?"

"I met this boss chick named Pam in the medical tent," Manny replies. "She took good care of me when I got cut."

"Very, very good care," I say.

"We got to rapping. Then her, her roommate, Mark and me went to dig some music and, after that we were like glue."

"Not Manny and me. Him and her."

"Like I was just telling my man, here, I'm going to move in with her in the city. See what develops."

"If your smile got any bigger," goes Lanie, "your cheeks would break."

"Mark, what's up with you?" River asks.

"The festival was dynamite. I feel good about it. But I'm with River, the O.M. can't rely on passing the hat and free rent to keep going."

"Clark ain't Wavy, Ava ain't Bonnie Jean," says River.

"In June, I got an offer to teach second grade in a ghetto school. All summer long, I've been trying to decide if working with kids is what I'm supposed to do, and right now, it feels exactly right. So that's what I'm going to do."

"Following your heart is always the right thing to do," says Lanie, as River and Manny nod.

We stand around awkwardly for a few seconds, then Manny stretches out his arms and we all enjoy a group hug.

Lanie says, "Come visit us in Taos."

"I'll give you my phone number in Brooklyn, you always have a place to stay," I say.

"I love you all," Manny says, "You're my amigos, my family."

HAPPY TRAILS

Tuesday, August 19, 1969

There's no way I can leave without saying goodbye to Dan the Man, so I bang on the office door and enter his construction office. Turning away from a desk stacked with paper, he smiles. "Can't believe it's over, it's unbelievable. Only one death, some poor guy in a sleeping bag got run over, and three births."

"Betcha in nine months, there's gonna be a whole lot of Woodstock babies being born. Music was a blast, but, for me, the crowd was the real deal."

Dan nods. "That's what I keep saying. Thanks to all you Hog Farmers, you people flew in here like angels and kept it all together."

"Actually, I came with the Ohayo Mountain Family. Tomorrow, I'm going back home to Brooklyn."

"Ever hear of Daytop Village?"

"The drug rehab joint?"

"There's one near here. The director called me to ask if we have any sheets, blankets, clothes. I go, 'Man, do we.' So he says they can use any we bring them, dirty don't matter."

"Before I drive another truck for you, I think I might have to join the Teamsters."

"Mark, it's easy. Just fill up the van with stuff and drop it off."

"Yeah, you're right. Why just throw it away."

"Tell you what, I'll sweeten the deal." Reaching in his pocket, "Twenty-five bucks to do it. Here's the directions."

"You got it."

I drive the van up the hill and park beside a huge pile of filthy stuff that's worth saving. Finding Dennis, I explain the mission, and he agrees to help load up the van and ride shotgun. With the roads back to near normal, the drive takes about a half hour. The director, a man with friendly smile and a big beard is outside the rehab. He directs us to the back where there are four industrial-sized laundry carts at the ready.

"Wish I cudda been there," says a guy with tattooed arms, who is helping to unload the van.

"Maybe next time," Dennis says.

"Ain't gonna be no next time," the guy growls. "They'll never get a lineup like that again?"

"Not only that," this chick chimes in. "But it was free, right?"

"Woodstock was a once in a lifetime thing," the guy says. "Sorry I missed it, is all."

When we finish unloading, the director thanks us and hands me a twenty. Driving back through the Village of White Lake, we stop at a luncheonette.

The waitress, middle-aged with teased blond hair, asks, "You from the festival?"

"Been there since last Monday," Dennis says. "Helped to set it up and now we're helping take it down."

"You kids were great."

The short order cook turns around, "I gotta admit it. Thought it would be a complete disaster and White Lake's name would be mud. But you came through with flying colors. You're OK in my book."

We thank them. When we go up to pay, the waitress says, "It's on us. But don't go telling the others."

Dennis finds a payphone on the street and makes a call. He returns to the van beaming. "Long story short—Maggie said she'll take me back."

"Hey, great."

"She didn't go into anything. Just said, 'Denny, I love you. Come home. We need you.'"

Back at the hub, the emptiness is eerie. Ava waves us over. "We have to get back to the house, there's a plumbing problem. Everyone's getting on the bus."

"Ava, I'm going to go back to Brooklyn. I'm got some kids I'm gonna teach. I figure I better start getting ready."

Dennis says, "I'm going back to Brooklyn, too."

Hugging each of us, Ava says, "You're both part of our family. You're always welcome at Ohayo Mountain."

Turning away, I find myself face to face with Candy. My heart's racing, but I tell myself to be cool.

"Howdy. You have a good time?" I ask.

"Totally groovy. How 'bout you?"

"There was this one little glitch at the beginning, my heart got knocked around a bit, but I'm OK now. Glad to have made your acquaintance."

"Serenity Book Shop. If you come to San Francisco, check us out. We jam every Wednesday night. I'll be there."

We hug. I hang on a just a tad too long, but so what.

"Happy trails."

"Happy trails."

On Tuesday morning, we hold our last yoga session. Wavy invites everyone to the Hog Farm.

Dennis rushes over to me. "I got us a ride."

"I'm ready. Let's go."